EPIC ATHLETES
LEBRON JAMES

Dan Wetzel
Illustrations by Setor Fiadzigbey

Henry Holt and Company
New York

For Jan

Henry Holt and Company, *Publishers since 1866*
Henry Holt® is a registered trademark of Macmillan Publishing Group, LLC
120 Broadway, New York, NY 10271 • mackids.com

Library of Congress Cataloging-in-Publication Data
Names: Wetzel, Dan, author.
Title: Epic athletes: LeBron James / Dan Wetzel.
Description: First edition. | New York : Henry Holt and Company, 2019. |
Audience: Ages: 8 to 12.
Identifiers: LCCN 2019002042 | ISBN 9781250295804 (hardcover)
Subjects: LCSH: James, LeBron—Juvenile literature. | Basketball players—
United States—Biography—Juvenile literature.
Classification: LCC GV884.J36 W4 2019 | DDC 796.323092 [B] —dc23
LC record available at https://lccn.loc.gov/2019002042

Our books may be purchased in bulk for promotional, educational, or business use.
Please contact your local bookseller or the Macmillan Corporate
and Premium Sales Department at (800) 221-7945 ext. 5442 or
by email at MacmillanSpecialMarkets@macmillan.com.

First edition, 2019 / Designed by Elynn Cohen

Printed in the United States of America
by LSC Communications, Harrisonburg, Virginia
1   3   5   7   9   10   8   6   4   2

1

The Block

EACH AND EVERY FAN, nearly twenty thousand in total, was on their feet inside Oracle Arena in Oakland, California. Standing in front of their seats. Standing on their seats. Standing in the aisles. They were too nervous to sit, after all.

With two minutes left in Game 7 of the 2016 NBA Finals, the Cleveland Cavaliers and the Golden State Warriors were tied 89–89. In addition to the twenty thousand in attendance, there were 44.5 million people tuned in to their televisions watching across America, and many millions more around the world.

While all those people were watching, LeBron James was searching—searching for a way to impact the game and seize a championship because he suddenly couldn't hit a jump shot. During the biggest moment of the biggest series, a series in which he'd averaged almost thirty points a game, LeBron couldn't make a basket.

In the final five minutes of the game, he missed from twenty-two feet, he missed from thirteen feet, he missed from two feet. He wasn't alone. The pressure was impacting everyone; the best players in the world were struggling with the intensity of the moment. LeBron's teammate Kyrie Irving had clanked a shot. So had fellow Cavalier Kevin Love. For the Warriors, Steph Curry had missed; so had Klay Thompson, Draymond Green, and Andre Iguodala.

Cleveland and Golden State had been battling for more than two and a half hours on this Father's Day. They had been going back and forth over nearly two weeks of this epic June championship clash. The action had been so even that not only was The Finals tied at three games apiece, and not only was this decisive game tied at 89, but at that very moment, each team had scored 699 cumulative points in the series. Everything was deadlocked.

Something had to give, though. There could only be one champion.

For LeBron, losing wasn't an option. He'd come too far to get to this point, to have this opportunity. He knew it meant too much to everyone not just back in Cleveland, but in all of Ohio, including the city of Akron, where he had grown up with a single mother and been a highly publicized star athlete since he was a kid.

He'd started his career with the Cavaliers in 2003 as the number one overall draft pick directly out of high school. He'd been crowned a basketball king before he ever stepped on a National Basketball Association (NBA) court and, by the age of eighteen, he'd already drawn comparisons to the legendary Michael Jordan, considered by many the greatest player of all time. But after seven seasons, even as he developed into the best player in the NBA, he couldn't win a championship. So, he left for Miami as a free agent.

Doing so angered fans back home in Ohio. They burned his jersey and cursed his name. They felt betrayed as he won two titles with the Miami Heat. Those should have been Cleveland's championships, they thought. Those should have been their victory parades, they complained.

LeBron didn't just win in Miami—more importantly, he learned *how* to win. He came to understand how it takes more than just scoring a lot of points and grabbing a lot of rebounds to become a champion. Winning requires sacrifice, teamwork, communication, and a mentality of doing whatever it takes—anything at all—to win, especially when you're losing.

It was a lesson he admits he didn't fully understand during his younger days with the Cavs. He said his four-year stretch in Miami was like "going off to college."

Older, wiser, and even more talented, he returned to Cleveland for the 2014–15 season, reigniting a love affair between himself and the fans in Northeast Ohio. He came back for one reason: to deliver that long-awaited championship to Cleveland. None of the city's three major professional sports teams had won a championship since 1964, when the Browns managed to win the National Football League title. By 2016, you needed to be well over the age of fifty to even remember it.

LeBron wanted to end that drought, or, as fans jokingly called it, the "curse." Cleveland is a blue-collar city of around 385,000 people and sits on Lake Erie. It is home to heavy industry, a major shipping port, and harsh winters. The city and its residents know what it's like to struggle. Unemployment. Crime. Poverty. Even jokes about its existence. In fact, back in 1969, the Cuyahoga River, which runs through the city, was so polluted with oil that it caught fire—literal burning water—and attracted insults and cracks from around America. Cleveland was dubbed the Mistake by the Lake.

The area wasn't a mistake for LeBron, though. It was simply home. Akron sits just over thirty miles to the south, almost a twin city for Cleveland, although smaller and poorer. And LeBron knew about overcoming the odds, about not accepting what others thought possible for you.

He was raised by a single teen mother, Gloria. His father was never around. His family was poor, accepting welfare to help buy food when his mom couldn't find work. They often couldn't afford to pay their rent, and were forced to move apartments in the city's toughest neighborhoods every few months before getting kicked out again. Sometimes, with nowhere else to go, they wound up sleeping on one of Gloria's friends' couches. All of LeBron's clothes and possessions fit into a single backpack. This was before he ever played organized sports or anyone saw him as a future NBA star.

In the fourth grade, LeBron was stuck living on

the other side of Akron from his elementary school. His mother didn't have a car, so it was a true struggle for him to find a ride to school in the mornings. He missed eighty-three days that year and was at risk of dropping out altogether even though he was just ten years old.

From that hopeless place, he rose.

And so regardless of how the outside world saw Northeast Ohio, LeBron knew this place. Yes, he knew the challenges. He also knew the positives, the success stories. He knew the good people in the community, the coaches and teachers who helped him and so many others. He knew his hometown's good times and happy stories, and the gorgeous summer sunsets. Mostly, he knew what a championship title, at last, would mean to his community.

In June of 2015, in his first season back in Cleveland, he led the Cavs to The Finals against Golden State. Injuries to star teammates Kyrie Irving and Kevin Love doomed them, though. The Warriors won four games to Cleveland's two. Now, twelve months later, it was a rematch.

Everyone on the Cavaliers was healthy and ready to prove they could be champions. It wouldn't be easy. Golden State had won a record seventy-three regular-season games and was considered possibly the greatest team in NBA history. Beating Curry, Thompson, and the rest of the Warriors felt at times like an impossible task. They had too many offensive weapons. Defensively they played with heart and toughness. When Golden State took a 3–1 series lead, many people wrote off Cleveland. After all, no team had ever come back from a 3–1 deficit in the NBA Finals, let alone against a seventy-three-victory defending champion set to play two of the three final games at home.

LeBron didn't care about the odds. His motto was about taking everything one possession at a time. In Game 5, facing elimination on the road in Oakland, both LeBron and Kyrie scored forty-one points and Cleveland stunned Golden State, 112–97. Then back in Cleveland for Game 6, LeBron again scored forty-one points, along with dishing eleven assists, as the Cavs won 115–101 to force Game 7.

Despite not being able to finish off the series quickly, Golden State still had confidence heading into Game 7. They still believed they were the best team, especially playing in front of their own fans, who were making a deafening noise cheering them on. Tied at 89, the game—and the championship— was still there for the taking.

With his jump shot failing him, LeBron knew he

needed to impact the game in ways other than just scoring. This was part of learning how to become a champion. Since LeBron couldn't score, the next best thing was to make sure Golden State couldn't either. This meant he had to play defense.

With 1:55 left in the tied game, Kyrie drove to the net and tried to throw up a running shot. It missed. Golden State's Andre Iguodala snatched the rebound out of the air and immediately turned up court. Four of the Cavaliers, including LeBron, Kyrie, and Love, were caught out of position. Iguodala immediately realized he had a nearly open court to attack. The only players in front of him were teammate Steph Curry and Cleveland's J. R. Smith.

In basketball terms, the Warriors had "numbers": a two-on-one fast break opportunity that might lead to an easy basket that could crush LeBron's dream of winning a title for Cleveland.

Iguodala began racing toward the basket, Curry following alongside him. J. R. Smith tried to back-pedal as fast as possible to play defense. The fans at Oracle began screaming in anticipation. Would this be the end, they wondered?

As Iguodala crossed midcourt he smartly passed it to Curry. That forced J. R. Smith to shift over to guard Curry. It was either that or allow Curry, the league's reigning Most Valuable Player, to go in for an easy layup. Just as Curry got the ball and saw Smith moving toward him, he sent a quick bounce pass back to Iguodala, who caught it in full stride. There was now no one between him and the potential championship-winning points.

Iguodala took two quick steps and leaped to the hoop, just past Smith, who tried to recover. A layup seemed inevitable. Then out of nowhere, an arm stretched over the shoulder of an unsuspecting Iguodala. Just as the possible title-winning shot was about to go in, LeBron James, with his head on the left side of the rim but his hand wrapped around to the right, flicked the shot away, coming in from behind at the last second.

"Blocked by James! LeBron James with the rejection," shouted the excited announcer on ESPN.

All over Oracle Arena, fans and players were in disbelief. Where had LeBron come from? How had he made that block?

LeBron had been way out of position when Iguodala first grabbed the rebound and headed up court for the two-on-one. Stuck deep on the far sideline, almost in the corner, LeBron decided he would find a way to make an impact.

"I was just like, 'Do not give up on the play,'"

LeBron told Cleveland.com. "If you've got an opportunity, just try to make this play."

LeBron James stands six foot eight and weighs around 255 pounds. He is extremely strong, yet plays with the speed of a man much lighter. But his best attribute as a player might be how he thinks about and sees the game—his basketball IQ. In this case, he instantly realized that Iguodala was going to pass it to Steph Curry, and Steph, being a smart player, would make the correct play and pass it back to give Iguodala a chance at the layup.

After processing all of that in an instant, LeBron put his head down and began sprinting powerfully not just back into the action, but exactly toward the spot on the court from which Iguodala would eventually attempt to score. He was a hunter, anticipating the path of his prey. Even the slightest hesitation would allow Iguodala to score. So LeBron went all out.

"'I can get it, I can get it,'" LeBron said he was thinking at the time. "I was like, 'J. R., don't foul him' and 'Bron, get the ball before it hits the backboard.'"

"Such a force," Golden State coach Steve Kerr marveled afterward.

In an instant, the entire NBA Finals changed

course. Golden State was stunned. Cleveland was energized. About a minute later, Kyrie hit a clutch three-pointer from the wing to make it 92–89. From there, Cleveland's defensive intensity continued as LeBron's teammates tried to match his ferocity. Steph missed two long three-pointers down the stretch, guarded tightly on each one. LeBron hit a free throw to extend the Cleveland lead to 93–89. Then Steph missed another three and Golden State's Marreese Speights missed a desperation shot at the buzzer. As the ball bounced helplessly away, LeBron began hugging his teammates.

Cleveland had won. At last, Cleveland was the champion.

"Just excitement," LeBron exclaimed. "Just excitement."

Growing up, LeBron had, like all young basketball players, dreamed of hitting the winning shot in Game 7 of the NBA Finals. In this case, though, the championship was won via defense, not offense. Golden State scored just thirteen points in the fourth quarter and none in the final 4:39 of the game. That was the difference. *That block* was the difference.

When the improbable, seemingly impossible, was done; when Cleveland's long, long-coveted title was won; LeBron simply fell to his knees and cried. This was his third NBA championship, but it didn't matter. He was still emotional.

He wept for the accomplishment. He wept for the comeback. He wept for all the energy he'd expired—averaging 36.3 points, 11.6 rebounds, and 9.7 assists while playing an average of almost forty-four minutes in the last three games, each of which were win-or-go-home contests for the Cavs.

He wept because Cleveland's fifty-two-year-old championship drought was over. He wept for Akron, his humble hometown. And he wept because he understood that a city that isn't glamorous and is often made fun of deserved to be a winner.

"Just knowing what our city has been through, Northeast Ohio has been through," LeBron said. "I came back for a reason. I came back to bring a championship to our city. I knew what I was capable of doing. Knew what I learned the last couple of years [while] I was gone. And I knew I had the right ingredients and the right blueprint to help this franchise get back to a place we've never been."

And all the sporting heartbreak, all the jokes, all the reminders of the oil-slicked burning Cuyahoga River? Cleveland was no longer a mistake.

"That's yesterday's newspaper," LeBron said. "I don't think anybody's reading yesterday's newspaper. They'll be reading tomorrow that I'm coming home. I'm coming home with what I said I was going to."

The trophy.

2
Growing Up

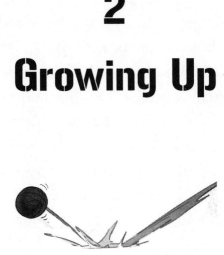

LEBRON RAYMONE JAMES was born December 30, 1984, in Akron, Ohio. He was the first and only child of Gloria James, who was just sixteen at the time of LeBron's birth. LeBron's father never married Gloria and was not involved in LeBron's life. He abandoned the family and offered no monetary or emotional support. It was mainly just LeBron and his mom, who hadn't finished high school and thus struggled to earn enough money to pay the bills.

At first LeBron and his mother lived in an old

home that their family had owned for generations, back to when it was part of a farm just outside downtown Akron. It needed repairs and sat on a dirt road, but there was a lot of family support. LeBron's grandmother Freda lived there and was able to watch over him as his mother tried to find work and continue her schooling. Money was still tight, but it worked. At least it did until Christmas 1987, when LeBron was about to turn three. Freda died of a heart attack that day, leaving Gloria in charge of not just her son, but two of her younger brothers, too.

Gloria was overwhelmed. As hard as she worked for her family, she lacked the education and skills to get a job that could support everyone, let alone childcare for LeBron. She mostly worked as a cashier at various shops. The family went on welfare, which provided a small check each month. The house quickly began to fall apart, with floorboards cracking in the living room and broken windows causing the cold air to blow in. By midwinter, the heating bill wasn't paid. Soon a neighbor, Wanda Reaves, discovered this young family sleeping in the cold, cavernous house. She offered to take them into her own home.

Realizing it was their best option, LeBron and his mom packed up what little they had and began sleeping together on Wanda's living room couch. The city soon condemned their old, now abandoned house, claiming it was a safety hazard. A bulldozer leveled it.

This began a period of uncertainty for LeBron and his mother. They were effectively homeless. They stayed for a little while with Wanda, but that couldn't be permanent. Mother and son began moving every few months, either staying with friends or relatives, or finding a cheap apartment for a brief stint.

"It was catch as catch can, scraping to get by," LeBron would write later in his autobiography, *Shooting Stars*. "My mom worked anywhere and everywhere, trying to make ends meet."

When LeBron was eight in the spring of 1993, the family moved five times in a three-month span. For LeBron, the constant moving and instability made him shy. It was difficult for him to trust people he didn't know. He'd look away when spoken to and kept his answers short. Making matters worse, he was always big for his age, so strangers sometimes assumed he was ten when he was really only six. They couldn't understand why he acted so immaturely, and naively questioned his intelligence.

He'd live in one place and attend one school for a spell, just long enough to make friends. Then he would suddenly move to a new place, often in a new neighborhood. While his teachers said he was a bright and dedicated student on the days he made it to class, he often missed school because he had no way to get there.

What LeBron lacked, like many kids in Akron and across America, was access to opportunities and a larger support system. That would start to change during the summer of 1993. One day, LeBron was outside a housing project where he and his mother were staying, playing with some other kids, when a man named Bruce Kelker pulled up in his car. Kelker coached a youth football team called the East Dragons and was looking for eight- and nine-year-olds to play for him.

"You guys like football?" Coach Kelker asked the kids, according to ESPN.

"That's my favorite sport," LeBron responded.

"How much football have you played?" Coach asked.

"None," LeBron answered.

Coach Kelker didn't mind. Most kids that age had never put on pads and, like LeBron, merely watched the game on television or threw the ball around with friends. LeBron had never played any organized sports. Not Little League. Not soccer. Not even basketball. His mother was too busy trying to survive. She didn't have extra money to pay for youth sports leagues.

A lot of boys in Akron were like that, which was why Coach Kelker was out looking for players instead of relying on their families to sign them up. He was eager to teach kids football. LeBron's mom wasn't in favor of him joining the team, but Coach Kelker wouldn't take no for an answer. He said the city recreation department would provide a helmet, shoulder pads, and all the equipment. He promised to come by every day and pick everyone up for practice.

That day he first met LeBron, Coach Kelker told the kids to line up for a footrace and whoever won would be his running back. LeBron beat everyone. With that, he was officially an East Dragon. Not long after, following a few weeks of practice to learn the basics, the East Dragons had their first game. On the first play, the quarterback handed the ball to

LeBron, who tucked it under his arm, burst through the line, and raced eighty yards for a touchdown. All over the field, coaches, players, and parents were amazed at his talent. It wouldn't be the last time he'd mesmerize a crowd.

After spending time with LeBron, Coach Kelker soon realized just how difficult his home life was. One day he would go to pick up LeBron for practice and discover LeBron and his mom had moved. Days later when he'd track them down at a new place, it would only be a matter of weeks—or even days—before they relocated again due to money problems.

Thinking he could help, Coach Kelker made Gloria an offer: Did she and LeBron want to come live with him temporarily? She took the deal.

With that decision, LeBron's life began to change. His mom became the team manager and would attend practices and games, where she began to love watching her son compete. LeBron scored nearly twenty touchdowns that season, and Gloria became famous in Akron for racing into the end zone to celebrate with her son each time.

Coach Kelker had no children and shared a small apartment with his girlfriend. There wasn't enough room for LeBron and his mother to stay there for long. As they began to wear out their welcome, another East Dragons coach stepped up with an idea.

Frankie Walker and his wife, Pam, felt bad LeBron was missing so much school. They didn't just see him as a gifted athlete. He was only nine years old, so the idea of playing pro football, or pro anything, was still a long shot. Education was different. The Walkers saw a smart kid who was painfully shy. They saw a kid who needed a stable base to build his life and they wanted to help.

"The Walkers were concerned that I was being passed from place to place, a nomad at age nine," LeBron wrote. LeBron was not getting in trouble. He was well behaved. Missing so many days of school in fourth grade put him at risk of never completing his education and making much out of his life, though.

"I was on the edge of falling into an abyss from which I could never escape," LeBron said.

The Walkers had a good-sized house in a comfortable neighborhood of Akron. They had three children, including a son, Frankie Jr., who was the same age as LeBron. Their plan called for LeBron to live with them during the week, assuring he would get hot meals and attend school daily, and then he'd stay with his mom on the weekends.

Moving in with the Walkers was a culture shock for LeBron. Some of it was great: There were family dinners; the heating and electric bills were always paid; he had the ability to relax and realize that he would be here for a bit and not face eviction or moving. For the first time in a long time LeBron had a bedroom to sleep in, which he shared with Frankie Jr. They even decorated it—hanging posters of NBA stars, such as Allen Iverson, on the wall.

Yet some of it required getting used to. The Walkers were disciplinarians and believed in raising their children with a strong work ethic and sense of responsibility.

Pam Walker would wake the children at 6:45 a.m. sharp for school. Manners were taught and enforced. Chores were a requirement—anything from helping clean the house, washing dishes, or doing yard work. Homework was to be finished. Always. They had to go to bed right at bedtime. There were no excuses for failing to live up to expectations. There was very little sitting around. LeBron gladly accepted the challenge and began to thrive.

"The Walkers laid a foundation for me," LeBron wrote. "The Walkers became family to me."

After missing all those days of school in the fourth grade, his fifth-grade experience was different. At Portage Path Elementary School that year, LeBron James had perfect attendance.

3

Akron

AKRON, OHIO, sits in the northeastern part of the state, around thirty miles south of Cleveland and Lake Erie, one of the Great Lakes. In the late 1800s, a number of rubber factories began springing up. Soon the city became known for its production of tires for the quickly growing automobile industry, and was dubbed the "Rubber Capital of the World." The population tripled from around sixty-nine thousand people in 1910 to two hundred and ten thousand in 1920.

Still, Akron never became a major city. It always

sat in the shadow of Columbus, the state capital, and Cleveland, which was bigger. Akron may have produced tires and shipped them around the globe, but few people came to the city or paid much attention to it. When LeBron was in grade school he would look at maps of the United States and notice dots for Cleveland and Columbus, but not Akron. It was like his hometown didn't exist. While he didn't know how, he vowed at the time to change that.

"I was going to let the world know where Akron was," LeBron wrote.

Football has long been the most popular sport in the area, with fans rabidly following not just the NFL's Cleveland Browns, but college football's Ohio State Buckeyes down in Columbus. The Pro Football Hall of Fame is in Canton, Ohio, less than twenty-five miles south of Akron. Local high schools built stadiums that routinely sat ten thousand and even fifteen thousand fans and many of the area's best players went on to star on college teams and in the NFL.

LeBron may have only been in grade school when he began playing for the East Dragons and later a different team called the South Rangers, but people around Akron had seen enough great players grow up there that they immediately suspected he might be capable of playing in college at least. His combination of size and speed was unique, and he seemed to truly love competing.

LeBron even heard adults talk about the possibility of him receiving a football scholarship that would allow him to attend college for free. He was young, but the message struck home. He was now mature enough to understand his situation in life. In school, he learned about the cycles of poverty that often prevent inner-city children, especially African Americans, from reaching their potential. No one from his family had attended college. No one talked about college, the way some middle- and upper-class families do. His mother hadn't even graduated from high school.

Although the idea of becoming a college graduate seemed almost impossible, he knew education was the key to rising out of poverty. "[I was] a statistic that was supposed to go the other way, growing up in the inner city, having a single-parent household," LeBron said. He was only in elementary school, but he promised himself he wouldn't let such an opportunity slip past him. He wanted to be the exception to the statistics. He began applying himself academically and later made the honor roll at Riedinger Middle School.

By that time, LeBron had already played some basketball, but mainly just with friends at the park. Then one day, he and Frankie were playing in the backyard, and Mr. Walker decided to make them play a game of one-on-one. LeBron had never been taught any fundamentals and was very raw. Frankie won that day, but Mr. Walker saw a lot of potential in LeBron.

"I could see LeBron really had something," Mr. Walker told *The Guardian*.

Mr. Walker also coached a basketball team, the Hornets, in a rec league at the Summit Lake Community Center. He put LeBron on the team and began working with him on the basics of the game, including ball handling and passing. LeBron was a natural. He already stood over five feet tall and wasn't just more athletic than the other kids. He also quickly realized that moving the ball around the court and playing as a team was the key to the game.

While playing rec ball that winter, LeBron caught the eye of a man named Dru Joyce II, who also coached basketball in the neighborhood. Coach Dru had a son, Dru Joyce III, who was the same age as

LeBron. The two knew each other from school and other activities. They were not friends.

Dru was a smaller kid, but he was a hard-nosed competitor who didn't allow anyone to intimidate him. Once, when LeBron and Dru were at the same church retreat, they got into a fight over a pillow. LeBron pushed Dru and figured Dru wouldn't do anything about it. He was wrong; Dru came up swinging and punched LeBron. A brief wrestling match ensued, but thankfully no one was hurt. From that point on, these two were at odds.

By the time they squared off in rec basketball, it was a full-on feud. Neither cared very much for the other, and each would get particularly amped for the matchup. Dru was short, but he was a great dribbler and passer, a natural point guard who could run the offense. He also played tough defense. LeBron was bigger and more naturally talented, but that didn't matter. When he played Dru and his team, it was serious business.

"Dru and LeBron were rivals," Coach Dru told a Cleveland television station years later.

Dru was also on a travel basketball team called the Shooting Stars. They didn't travel far, usually just around the Akron area or maybe as far as Cleveland.

When a few players quit the team, the coach needed to fill out the roster.

Coach Dru, having seen LeBron play, stepped in. "I know a guy you might want," he told the Shooting Stars' coach.

While LeBron and Dru hadn't liked each other up until this point, now that they were teammates they became fast friends. They were actually very similar—neither one wanted to lose at anything. That's why they clashed. "We were both very competitive," LeBron said. And that's also why they jelled on the basketball court. Dru was nicknamed "The General" because he would shout out orders to teammates and hold them accountable when they made mistakes. He was famous for playing one-on-one games and demanding rematches if he lost. It didn't matter if he lost five or ten in a row; he'd keep playing until he won.

By the following fall, LeBron's fifth-grade year, the coach of the Shooting Stars had quit. Coach Dru, even though he didn't have much experience in basketball, took over. Coach Dru wasn't just a basketball coach for LeBron, he became a mentor—even a surrogate dad at times.

Coach Dru had graduated from Ohio University and worked as a senior sales representative and businessman. He could have moved to a fancier neighborhood, but liked the west side of Akron and wanted to give back to the community. He impressed everyone with his intelligence and class, and maintained an understanding of the kind of life kids born into single-parent homes in the area dealt with.

The Shooting Stars practiced inside an old, linoleum-floored gym at a local Salvation Army. Coach Dru would run the team through drills, trying to pound home the fundamentals of the game. He didn't know much about how the Amateur Athletic Union (AAU) worked, but he sensed he had a special group of players. The team wasn't just talented; they got along really well. Dru was a perfect point guard and leader. Then there was a big kid named Sian Cotton who was raw, but willing to work and learn. LeBron was so skilled his potential seemed limitless.

"Everything kind of mushroomed after that," Coach Dru said.

They started winning right away and qualified for the AAU under-11 national championships in Cocoa Beach, Florida. The team raised money, rented a van, and headed to Florida. For most of the players, it was their first trip outside of Ohio and first time seeing the ocean.

The tournament was intimidating. There were teams from all over the country. They had fancy uniforms and matching sneakers due to sponsorship deals with Nike or Adidas. Some teams represented entire states or regions, or came from major cities with much wider talent pools, such as the Southern California All-Stars, Brooklyn USA, the Michigan Mustangs, and the Atlanta Celtics. The Shooting Stars predominantly hailed from the same neighborhood of the same small city.

Uniforms and zip codes didn't matter once the ball was tipped, though. LeBron and his teammates shook off the initial intimidation and just played their game. Dru set up the offense. Siam and LeBron took care of the scoring. Everyone played defense and took pride in showing the kids from around the country that Akron had good players, too. There were sixty-four teams in the tournament and the Shooting Stars wound up finishing ninth. It was a long way from a national title, but it was better than they'd expected.

"I don't know what it is," Coach Dru told the team after, "but you guys are going to do something special."

The trip to Florida had done more than increase

the Shooting Stars' confidence. It sparked a dream. If as a new team they could come in ninth place, then how much better would they do with some additional years of playing and practicing together? As they made the long, thousand-plus-mile drive home, they talked about winning a national championship. It quickly became an obsession.

Later the Shooting Stars would add another piece to the puzzle—a tough, athletic kid named Willie McGee. Willie had been born and partially raised in a dangerous neighborhood in Chicago. As a way of dodging trouble, he played basketball, dribbling a ball nearly everywhere he went. When his older brother enrolled at the University of Akron, Willie's mother decided Willie would be safer living with his brother in Akron. Willie was tall, six foot two as a sixth grader, and very good at basketball. He was just the addition the team needed.

With that, the Shooting Stars' core was in place: Dru, Sian, Willie . . . and LeBron James.

They eventually began calling themselves the Fab Four.

The Shooting Stars became more than just a basketball team to LeBron. They became family. After spending his early years moving from home to home, school to school, and neighborhood to neighborhood, he now craved consistency in life. Having to constantly make new friends or adjust to new environments had pushed him to shyness. Now it felt like his life was turning a corner.

Around this same time, through a rental-assistance program, the Walkers and some other families helped Gloria find a modest, two-bedroom apartment at the nearby SpringHill Apartments. It wasn't much. It was designed for and filled with low-income tenants and could be dangerous, especially at night. Still, there was a sense of stability. LeBron was back living with his mom. He had his own room. It was their place.

"All of it felt good," LeBron wrote. "All of it felt right. But without the time I spent at the Walkers', I don't honestly know what would have become of me."

Later in life, LeBron would create a Hollywood production company. He named it SpringHill Entertainment as a reminder of the place where he would lie in his bedroom and dream of the future. With his home life more stable, LeBron found additional comfort in his basketball team. The players began to grow close and spend time hanging around the Joyces' house, playing *Madden NFL*, watching TV, or listening to music.

"I wanted to finally have some brothers that I could be loyal to," LeBron said in the documentary *More Than a Game*.

LeBron continued to play football, but basketball took up much of his time. The Shooting Stars would play 60–70 games a year, traveling around Ohio, the entire Midwest, and even the country. The Fab Four began developing an on-court chemistry to match their off-court friendship.

A year after finishing ninth at the AAU tournament, the team traveled to Salt Lake City, Utah, for another run at the national championship. They came in tenth—still a good performance—but short of their high expectations. They wanted to win it all. The next year they tried again, this time in Memphis, Tennessee, but did poorly. This was mainly because the guys had spent too much time playing in the motel pool and, in Coach Dru's opinion, not enough time focusing on winning. Coach Dru was not pleased. On the long drive home he lectured the boys, telling them it didn't matter how talented they thought they were. To succeed, they had to put in the work.

The Shooting Stars took the lesson to heart. The following summer, in 1999, as eighth graders, they believed they were capable of winning the AAU national title. Since summer basketball is different for high school–age players, it was likely LeBron would play for a different team in the future. That meant it was now or never for the Shooting Stars.

The event was in Orlando, Florida, at a huge sports complex on the campus of Disney World. There was no fooling around this time. The Shooting Stars saw this as a business trip. They beat a team from Illinois by thirty-five. They pounded a team from South Carolina by forty. The Fab Four was playing better and better. LeBron was now over six feet tall. Sian's game had developed to make him a powerful scorer and rebounder. Willie could do it all and brought confidence to the team. And then there was Dru, who was still so small everyone underestimated him . . . until he dribbled right around them.

The team entered the knockout stage of play, where a single loss would send them home. They were playing the best players and teams in the country, so it wouldn't be easy. They beat a team from Kansas City by fourteen points in round one. Then they survived a tight one against a Florida club, 65–62.

The year before they had been knocked out of the tournament by the Missouri Skywalkers. This time they got revenge, winning 71–59.

They won in the quarterfinals by sixteen and the semifinals by seventeen. They were crushing the competition and just one victory away from what they had worked so hard to achieve—a national title.

In their path, however, were the Southern California All-Stars, a team featuring most of the best players from Los Angeles. The Southern California All-Stars had won the AAU national title in each of the last three years, as fifth, sixth, and seventh graders. They had a six-foot-five center and a power forward who was just a little shorter. There was a guard who was six-one who could fly through the air and dunk. Akron had around two hundred thousand residents at the time. Los Angeles had twenty million, meaning they had a much larger talent pool to pick from. It didn't seem fair.

The Shooting Stars wondered if they could beat a team with so many good players. When the game started, they played scared, falling behind by fifteen points. It looked like the kids from Akron were going to be humiliated.

That's when the team got together and decided

they wouldn't allow it. If nothing else, they were going down fighting. Yes, there are a lot more people in California, a lot more potential star athletes, but only five can play on the court at a time.

With that attitude adjustment, the Shooting Stars started to hold their own, and then slowly cut into the lead. They soon got it down to single digits. Then down to five. LeBron began to take over on offense. Sian and Willie were locking it down on defense. The Southern California All-Stars began to get rattled. They hadn't been challenged like this in a long time, if ever.

With four seconds left, the Shooting Stars got the ball. They trailed by just two points. Coach Dru called a time-out and set up a play. They would inbound it to LeBron and give him a chance to either win or tie the game and secure a national title for Akron. LeBron knew he was ready. He had proven himself to be one of the best players in the country. Everyone respected his game, including all these kids from Los Angeles.

LeBron received the pass, but was guarded tightly by a defender. He dribbled to open up some space, but with time quickly draining from the clock, he knew he had to shoot from deep. Around thirty-five feet from the basket, but with a clear view of the hoop, he let a three-point attempt fly. To LeBron it looked like it was going in for the victory. He could practically imagine the celebration, the joy he'd share with the rest of the Fab Four and his other team-mates, the pride of returning home with the trophy.

Then it hit the rim. It rattled around. It popped out.

The California All-Stars celebrated. The North-east Ohio Shooting Stars were devastated. They'd come so close. But not close enough. They were runners-up. Coach Dru tried to comfort them, but the loss stung. It remains a shot that LeBron regrets missing to this day.

At the time, the Fab Four thought their chance at winning a national title together was over, forever.

They must've forgotten that high school was just around the corner.

1:54

4

St. Vincent-St. Mary

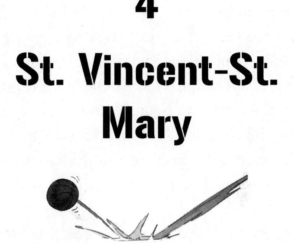

IN SEVENTH GRADE, Dru heard about a basketball clinic being offered every Sunday night at the Jewish Community Center in West Akron. It was run by Keith Dambrot, who used to coach Division I college basketball at Central Michigan University. Coach Dambrot had grown up in Akron and played baseball at the University of Akron. He was back living in town and working as a financial planner. He still wanted to coach, though, so he began offering weekly clinics to kids who were looking to learn the game. It only cost one dollar to participate in each clinic.

Despite being so small, Dru wanted to play college basketball. He thought the chance to learn from a former college coach would help him reach his goal. Since LeBron did just about everything Dru did, soon enough they were both attending the clinic. Coach Dambrot was definitely a great coach; he put them through rigorous drills each week, especially dribbling and shooting with their left hands, which would make them more difficult to defend. It was slow going, but it was fun. LeBron felt like he was improving.

Like most kids on Akron's west side, LeBron assumed that he would attend a public school called Buchtel High. Dru was going to go there, too, along with Sian and Willie. Coach Dru had even been hired as an assistant basketball coach with the hope that he would help draw in the Fab Four.

LeBron became particularly famous in the neighborhood when in eighth grade his team played a fun basketball game against the teachers at Riedinger Middle School. It was an annual event and the teachers, being grown-ups, usually won. Not this time, though, especially when LeBron got free on a fast break. He leaped through the air, reached high, and got the basketball just over the rim and in. It was a dunk, his first ever in actual competition. His fellow students went wild in the stands. "[My classmates] were like, 'What did you just do?'" LeBron said in a Disney special years later. "I was like, 'I have no idea.'" The students went on to beat the teachers, 71–39.

As word spread of these up-and-coming, talented young kids, people at Buchtel began envisioning state championships.

Then something unexpected occurred. When LeBron was in eighth grade, Coach Dambrot was hired as the head basketball coach at St. Vincent-St. Mary, a private Catholic school just west of downtown. It was a prestigious college preparatory school. Even though it was located only a couple of miles from where LeBron lived, he'd never before considered going there. Almost no one from his neighborhood did. It was a school for wealthy suburban kids, or at least that's how the people of his neighborhood saw it.

The hiring of Coach Dambrot changed everything. Suddenly there was a chance for the Fab Four to attend a very strong academic school and play for a coach who could prepare them for college and beyond. The school offered financial aid, and LeBron and some of the others would certainly qualify.

Dru wanted to go to SVSM, as the school is known, even though his dad was coaching at Buchtel. Since Dru was always a leader, Sian, Willie, and LeBron all agreed to follow him.

The decision was controversial. A lot of people in their neighborhood felt the Fab Four were abandoning the community by choosing a private school. Meanwhile, Coach Dambrot hired Coach Dru as an assistant, since he had coached the Fab Four in AAU ball. That meant Coach Dru was also criticized for selling out. But ultimately, LeBron and his friends chose to ignore all the talk and agreed to do what they thought was best for each of their futures.

After enrolling, the biggest adjustment wasn't even athletics. The guys knew their play on the court would take care of itself. But getting accustomed to the school's culture was challenging.

The Fab Four had always attended public city schools, where the student bodies were mostly made up of African American kids. SVSM was a Catholic school that drew students from all over Akron and its suburbs. The vast majority were white and many came from families that earned a great deal of money. LeBron had rarely spent any time with white kids or rich kids before. His neighborhood was all

African American and almost all were low-income or working-class families.

On top of that change, LeBron was nervous and standoffish. Entering any high school, even a familiar one, can be intimidating for a freshman. This was an entirely new world. LeBron wasn't sure the white students even wanted him in the school. He didn't know what to think or whom to trust.

"When I first went to the ninth grade in high school, I was like, 'I'm going to this school to play ball and that's it,'" LeBron said years later on the HBO show *The Shop*: "'I don't want [anything] to do with white people. I don't believe they want anything to do with me. Me and my boys, we're going to high school together and we're here to hoop.' Those were my initial thoughts and my initial shock to white America when I was fourteen years old."

That mindset would soon fade as he realized the school was far more welcoming than he expected. LeBron, Sian, and Willie all played football as freshmen and immediately met a bunch of new classmates and made friends. They got the same reaction in class, where the tough academics made it so everyone needed someone to lean on for support. LeBron may have thought the other kids didn't want him there, but in reality they were happy that everyone was going through the challenges they were. It didn't matter what color anyone's skin was or what neighborhood they came from.

"It took me a little while to kind of adjust to it," LeBron said.

SVSM was tough for everyone. There was a dress code requiring students to wear dress shoes and collared shirts tucked into slacks with black or brown belts. There could be no piercings, braids, or facial hair. Tattoos had to be covered up. LeBron had been used to wearing whatever he wanted, whenever he wanted. Now he was dressing . . . preppy.

Then there were the strict school rules. You couldn't be late for class. You had to be quiet in the classrooms. Unexcused absences were not tolerated. You were there to learn and prepare for college. Everything was about discipline and order.

Academically, LeBron had to make up some ground among his classmates. Many had attended private elementary and middle schools. Their parents had money to hire tutors when coursework was challenging, or they were college graduates themselves and could help with homework. LeBron never had access to any of that. He started ninth grade with academic experience that was closer to a seventh-grade level. He needed to adapt. Quickly. Through hard work and a love of learning, he achieved, pushing himself to make the honor roll.

"I actually liked the schoolwork," LeBron later wrote.

Helping ease the adjustment was the presence of an older kid and one of the few students who also came from LeBron's neighborhood. His name was Maverick Carter. He was a senior, not to mention the captain and star of the basketball team. LeBron was five years old when he first met Maverick, who was smart, outgoing, and charismatic. LeBron and his friends looked at Maverick and saw someone they wanted to emulate. If he had come from their neighborhood and been successful, then maybe so could they.

As LeBron started to find his footing at SVSM that fall, he made his varsity football debut for the Fighting Irish despite being only a freshman. While he had shown potential playing for the junior varsity team, no one was certain he could handle the next level. He stood around six foot three and weighed one hundred and seventy pounds. He was fast, could jump high, and had huge hands to grab the ball. In the final game of the SVSM season, the Fighting Irish were struggling to score. LeBron was in uniform on the sideline, but wasn't expecting to play.

That's when the coach decided to put him in, hoping to spark the offense. LeBron immediately made his presence felt, snagging balls out of the air and out-leaping defensive backs. SVSM lost that day, 15–14, but LeBron caught two touchdown passes. Everyone was buzzing about how good he was— and how good he could become.

When basketball season began, there would be no one wondering if he would play for the varsity team. Coach Dambrot recognized his talent and knew he belonged on the A team. First, though, LeBron had to make it through practice. During those Sunday night clinics, Coach Dambrot had been a mild-mannered teacher of the game. He liked keeping things light and fun while trying to improve every kid who showed up.

At SVSM, his style was completely different. Coach Dambrot was back to acting like a college coach. He screamed. He shouted. He put the players through endless wind sprints and drills. He demanded things were done perfectly or the players would have to do them again. LeBron couldn't believe it at first. This didn't even seem like the same person. That nice guy running clinics was gone. In his place was a demanding coach who believed in making sure the team was one hundred percent ready when the season started.

"When you're prepared you have a lot of confidence going into a game," LeBron said. "[When] I was a freshman we were well prepared. We had a great high school coach."

The Fighting Irish's first game was at Cuyahoga Falls High School, a big suburban school north of Akron. It had around twice as many students as SVSM. Its gymnasium could seat as many as thirty-five hundred people. LeBron had played in many AAU games, but those rarely attracted any fans. Its spectators were just friends and family, even for the national championship.

All day leading up to the game, LeBron was anxious. He'd actually been anxious all week. He'd dreamed of this night for a long time, his first varsity game. As a kid he often attended Buchtel High School games and saw those older kids as heroes. There were no pro sports teams in Akron, so everyone followed the high schools. Now he was going to be one of them, out on the court.

As the team warmed up, he looked at all those rows of bleachers filling up and tried to remind himself he'd be fine. He could do this. He was a good player. He was still just fourteen years old, though.

"I was nervous," LeBron later told the Cleveland *Plain Dealer*. "Like, scared nervous, shaking nervous . . . making that jump from middle school to high school is just as big of a jump for someone as going into the NBA. Because when you look at the other kids, some of them were three years older than me. That was the first time I'd experienced that. They were bigger and more confident."

He had nothing to worry about.

Early in the game, he got free on a fast break and scored on a layup. Then he got another. He slowly settled in. Maverick helped calm everyone down and showed a lot of leadership. SVSM rolled to a victory, 76–40. LeBron scored fifteen points and grabbed eight rebounds. Dru came off the bench and hit a three-pointer, despite being barely five feet tall and weighing around one hundred pounds. The whole team thrived, and with that, the season was on.

The next night they beat Cleveland Central

Catholic and LeBron had twenty-one points and seven rebounds. After that, the victories just kept coming. As did LeBron's show-stopping play. He had twenty-one against Cleveland's Benedictine High School and eighteen against Redford High School from Detroit, Michigan. By the end of December, he was averaging 19.0 points a game and SVSM was 7–0. He scored twenty-one on his fifteenth birthday. It was clear to everyone this was no ordinary freshman.

SVSM kept playing and SVSM kept winning. The Irish record got to 10–0, then 15–0, then 20–0. Coach Dambrot never let up in practice, pushing for better and better no matter how many games they won. At the state playoffs, the guys were dreaming about reaching the finals in Columbus, which would be played at the nineteen-thousand-seat arena on the campus of Ohio State University. The reality was that even a single loss could end their season.

"We were prepared," LeBron said. "So, we went out and just let it happen. Let it play, and let it play out."

How it played out was a series of blowout victories by SVSM, in which they won by thirty-six, seventeen, eighteen, and then thirty-three. The closest game was a seven-point victory in the quarterfinals. In the semis, SVSM won again behind LeBron's nineteen points and eleven rebounds. LeBron had gone from being nervous about playing high school basketball to dominating it.

The state finals were played all day long, with games running back-to-back featuring teams from all the different divisions from all corners of the state. Around thirteen thousand fans were in attendance, by far the biggest crowd LeBron had ever played before. Many of them were specifically there to see him. Word of this spectacular freshman and his undefeated team from Akron had made its way throughout the state.

The opponent was Greeneview High School, a team from southwest Ohio. LeBron would score twenty-five points, but the story of the game was Dru, who went seven for seven from three-point range and scored twenty-one. The crowd couldn't believe this little kid could be so good, but LeBron and the others already knew.

It was enough to give SVSM a 73–55 victory to take the championship and finish the season with a record of 27–0. LeBron was named MVP of the state tournament and first team All-Ohio, which meant he was already one of the best players in the state, if not the best.

The year before, SVSM had lost in the quarter-finals. Now they were unbeatable.

And they were just getting started.

5

Big Dreams

IT'S RARE FOR A freshman to even make the varsity roster, let alone play, let alone start, let alone star, let alone be named MVP of the state tournament on an undefeated championship team.

Yet as great as LeBron's basketball career was going, he still wanted to play football, the sport he first loved. The fall of his sophomore season, LeBron became a full-time starting wide receiver.

He was almost unstoppable. He was nearly six foot seven by then, yet could still sprint as fast as anyone. Quarterbacks would throw a pass high in the air and he would leap over defenders and grab it. Or they would throw it deep and he would run under and catch it. His hands were huge. His coordination was incredible. He caught forty-two passes for 820 yards and scored seven touchdowns as a sophomore. He was named All-State. A year later, he caught sixty-one passes for 1,245 yards and scored sixteen touchdowns. He was named All-State again.

It was enough for college football programs to take notice, and suddenly LeBron was receiving recruiting offers from all over—Ohio State University, Florida State University, even the University of Southern California all the way out in Los Angeles. Many football coaches figured LeBron could easily reach the NFL. The defensive coordinator for SVSM was a man named Mark Murphy, who played eleven seasons as a defensive back and safety for the NFL's Green Bay Packers. He compared LeBron as a wide receiver to a guy he played against in the NFL— Jerry Rice, a Hall of Famer and the all-time leader in receptions and touchdown receptions.

LeBron was *that* good.

College football coaches would regularly come to LeBron's high school looking to recruit him. One day a young assistant coach from the University of Notre Dame traveled to see LeBron. His name was

Urban Meyer. Meyer didn't know much about LeBron the basketball player. He had studied tape of LeBron the football player, though. Meyer found LeBron in the hallway and invited him to visit Notre Dame's campus. LeBron was polite and grateful, but seemed more surprised than interested. He thought everyone knew his future was in the NBA, not playing college football. Meyer later asked the SVSM football coach what was up since players are usually excited to hear from a powerhouse such as Notre Dame. The SVSM coach began laughing.

"'You don't know who that is?'" Meyer later recalled the coach saying. "'That's the next Michael Jordan.'"

Indeed, by the middle of high school, a lot of people were calling LeBron the next Michael Jordan. Jordan was considered the greatest basketball player of all time after leading the Chicago Bulls to six NBA titles. He even became the face of his own Nike sneaker brand called Air Jordan. LeBron didn't know if he'd ever really be that good, but he was determined to find out.

After injuring his wrist playing hoops before his senior year, LeBron even gave up football. His basketball career was too valuable to risk. One rough tackle could cost him everything. To this day, he still loves football and wonders what might have been. And he's a big Ohio State fan, regularly attending games in Columbus, where, in the past, he'd reconnected with a familiar face . . . Urban Meyer, who was the Buckeyes' longtime head coach until he retired in late 2018.

In terms of basketball, everything began happening fast for LeBron. After Maverick graduated following the Fighting Irish's state championship win, LeBron became the team leader his sophomore season. Dru, Sian, and Willie all began playing bigger roles, too. There was also a new member of the group, a kid named Romeo Travis who was six foot six and had played as a freshman at Central Hower High School, just across town from SVSM. The Fab Four already knew Travis from playing against him in middle school. He was a tough player who never backed down.

While they were once rivals, now they were teammates. It didn't take long before a friendship was built out of respect. The Fab Four became a five-man group as Coach Dambrot put together a schedule with fewer local opponents and more games against the best teams in the country. SVSM was too good for just Ohio competition. They wanted to play, and beat, everyone.

That old AAU goal of winning a national championship now became the goal for St. Vincent-St. Mary. Every week, *USA Today* publishes a ranking of the best high school teams in the country. LeBron and his friends began obsessing about it. If they could win every game against a better schedule than the previous year's, they could finish at the top and finally bring that national title to Akron.

It wouldn't be easy. The *USA Today* rankings are generally dominated by schools in major cities like New York, Chicago, or Los Angeles. Then there was an elite team that often topped the rankings, Oak Hill Academy, a small boarding school in Virginia with a legendary coach named Steve Smith. His program is so well-known that many of the best players in the country transfer there, moving away from their families to focus on academics and improving their game. Through the years, Oak Hill has won nine national titles and featured hundreds of upcoming college stars and dozens of future NBA players, including All-Stars Kevin Durant and Carmelo Anthony. In national high school basketball, no one had a bigger team than Oak Hill. No one.

St. Vincent-St. Mary was just a team made up of some guys who'd grown up together. As LeBron and his friends scanned the newspaper each week, defeating Oak Hill seemed like an impossible dream.

LeBron's sophomore season opened against one of the new, tougher opponents that Coach Dambrot had scheduled—Cape Henry Collegiate, a power-house from Virginia Beach, Virginia, that boasted two future college players. This was supposed to be a test.

Instead, they proved to be no match for the Fighting Irish. LeBron scored twenty-three and SVSM won big, 74–38. Three nights later, LeBron scored thirty-four against Akron's Garfield High School. They went on to beat top teams from Michigan, Wisconsin, and Pennsylvania. Soon SVSM was 9–0 and ranked third in the *USA Today* poll.

Up next was the number one team in the nation . . . Oak Hill Academy.

The game was played in Columbus as part of a tournament of some of the best high school teams in America. This was what SVSM had been waiting for—a chance to truly prove themselves nationally. If they won, they'd have the inside track on a national championship.

Oak Hill was atop the rankings for a reason, though. They were led by a seven-foot center named

DeSagana Diop who hailed from Senegal and later that year would be a top draft pick of the Cleveland Cavaliers. The other four starters would all eventually play Division I college basketball and had come to Oak Hill from Atlanta, Baltimore, and New Jersey. Oak Hill was loaded.

While LeBron had mostly gotten over being nervous on the court, this game reminded him of that first start as a freshman. Through AAU ball, he had played against or seen most of the guys on Oak Hill, but this was still *Oak Hill Academy*, not just some team from Dayton or Toledo. Whatever nerves he had, he overcame them, scoring thirty-three points despite the high level of competition.

In the final seconds of the game, Oak Hill led 79–78, but SVSM had the ball. Coach Dambrot called a play for LeBron to shoot. Hit this and a national title was possible. Hit this and no one could deny that a group of guys from Akron could take on any high school in America. LeBron got the ball on the perimeter and hoisted up a nineteen-footer. It looked good. Then it wasn't.

Clank.

Once again LeBron missed the final shot and felt crushed. Oak Hill celebrated. They had survived.

They'd go on to finish the season 33–0 and be crowned *USA Today*'s national champion. Again.

But they wouldn't forget that night against LeBron. "[LeBron's] a special player, you aren't going to see many like him," Oak Hill Coach Steve Smith said to reporters after the game. "He took it to us."

While disappointed, nearly defeating Oak Hill filled the guys with confidence. It wasn't just the realization that LeBron might be the best high school player in the country despite being just a sophomore. It was how Dru and Sian and Willie and Romeo had played, too. If they could play with the same intensity against everyone else, they'd be hard to beat.

And they were. The next big game on the schedule came a few weeks later. This one didn't feature some out-of-state opponent or a school filled with players from all over the country. It was a rivalry game against Buchtel, the west side public school most of the guys chose not to attend so they could go to SVSM. They knew all the kids at Buchtel, and they knew Buchtel was eager to beat SVSM and show LeBron and the others that they'd made a mistake choosing SVSM.

The game was intense. The Buchtel players gave everything they had, but LeBron scored thirty-three and SVSM won again. They'd sweep the rest of their regular-season schedule on the way to a 19–1 regular-season record, and then cruise through the playoffs, defeating Miami East High, a school not too far from Dayton, in the finals. LeBron was named MVP of the state tournament. He was also named not just Mr. Basketball in the State of Ohio, which goes to the best player in the state, but first team All-American by *USA Today*. He averaged 25.3 points and 7.4 rebounds a game.

He was still just a sophomore.

6

National Stardom

As SOON AS LeBron's sophomore high school season ended, he began playing for an AAU team in California named the Oakland Soldiers. The Shooting Stars were no longer together. LeBron was now on what basketball fans call the circuit, where the very best players in America travel around the country playing in tournaments and participating in talent camps. The Soldiers were a major team in that world.

One day, the Soldiers had a scrimmage set up in the gym at the University of San Francisco. They were going to take on some local college players.

While the game would offer some good competition, it was scheduled for a single reason—a chance for LeBron to be scouted by a man named Sonny Vaccaro.

If LeBron was the would-be king of basketball, then Sonny was the kingmaker. Sonny worked for the shoe company Adidas. His job was to find future NBA stars and build relationships with them so he might get them to sign endorsement deals with Adidas.

Back in 1984, when he worked at Nike, Sonny scouted and signed Michael Jordan. It led to one of the richest shoe deals in history; the Jordan brand still dominates sales years after Michael retired from basketball. In 1996, Sonny signed Kobe Bryant to Adidas. Now Sonny had been told the next big thing would be playing in San Francisco and he needed to see this kid to believe it.

Sonny took a seat and eyed LeBron, who was now around six foot seven and 215 pounds. The way LeBron ran and jumped was unheard of for his size and age. Throughout four decades, Sonny had scouted thousands of players. He was an expert in identifying talent, not just if a player would be good or even great, but if a player could be truly special—the kind who would make kids and adults around the world want to wear their trademark sneakers.

The game began and LeBron immediately showed he was that kind of star. He had no nerves about performing before a man who had the power to make him fabulously wealthy. Sonny watched with mouth open as LeBron ran the court, drained shots, and sent in powerful dunks. Then LeBron grabbed a rebound over a bigger player, took a couple of dribbles up court like a guard, and promptly whipped a long bounce pass through two defenders to a streaking teammate for an easy basket.

In one play he'd shown strength, determination, speed, skill, coordination, and a rare vision of the court. Sonny was stunned. He thought he'd seen it all. Then he saw LeBron.

"I'll never forget that pass," Sonny said. "The thing [was] everyone knew he was playing for an audience. Whenever a kid plays for an audience, and I've done this a few times, they try to [impress] by scoring. They hit three jumpers in a row and then they come down talking. They're kids."

Yet rather than try to impress Sonny Vaccaro by scoring a lot of points, LeBron was comfortable just passing the ball and playing the game the right way.

"That's when I knew," Sonny said. "That's when I said, 'This is it.'"

Sonny watched for a few more minutes and then walked outside the gym to call a high school coach he worked with in New York City.

"I just saw the greatest high school player I've ever seen," Sonny said.

With that, LeBron James was no longer just any high school player. He was about to become a very big star. Sonny and his wife, Pam, flew to Akron to meet with LeBron and his mom. While LeBron couldn't legally receive any money from Adidas yet, Sonny signed St. Vincent-St. Mary to an endorsement deal, supplying the basketball team with new uniforms, dozens and dozens of new Adidas shoes, and warm-up gear. In addition to the swag, Adidas also paid SVSM fifteen thousand dollars to help pay for travel expenses.

With the Adidas marketing machine behind him, suddenly LeBron was being interviewed by major newspapers and TV stations like ESPN and Fox Sports. He even appeared on the cover of *Sports Illustrated*! It declared him "The Chosen One" and said, "High school junior LeBron James would be an NBA lottery pick right now."

LeBron had blown up nationally. His life was forever changed.

"Sonny did so much for me," LeBron said. "He made so much of this possible."

There was immediate backlash, of course. Some people doubted LeBron could really be that good.

Was he good? Sure, they assumed. But could he really be a top draft pick as a high school junior? Others thought all of the attention and hype LeBron received would go to his head, especially because he was so young and inexperienced.

"Just about every major NBA writer, every TV type ripped me and LeBron," Sonny said. "They doubted his ability. I just felt bad for them. They hadn't seen him and they just acted like they had. If you had seen him, you couldn't say that. They also didn't know him. If you knew him, you knew he would continue to work hard. They didn't know what they were talking about."

The summer between LeBron's sophomore and junior seasons, he attended Sonny's prestigious talent camp, ABCD. It featured around one hundred of the best players in America. Many of them were a year older than LeBron. Almost every major college coach, NBA scout, and NBA coach attended the camp to scope out the young talent.

LeBron was the one everyone wanted to see. Could he handle the pressure? Could he deal with this level of competition? Was he legit?

Also attending the camp was a six-foot-six player named Lenny Cooke. He played high school ball in Brooklyn and was considered a legend in New York City. Many of the local New York papers thought Lenny was the best player in America. He was older, already nineteen, but still in high school. He had long arms and a smooth way of gliding on the court.

Everyone at the camp was excited to watch the game between Lenny's team and LeBron's team. This was a showdown. LeBron wasn't nervous, though. He liked the attention and competition. LeBron began draining jumpers and driving to the basket. Then late in the game, LeBron stripped the ball from Lenny, took it down the court, and dunked it to seal a victory for his team. He had clearly outplayed the supposed number one player in the country. Lenny was a good player, but LeBron was a truly great one. Even the New York newspapers had to admit LeBron was the best.

When LeBron returned to SVSM for his junior

season, there was a major change awaiting him. Coach Dambrot had been hired as an assistant coach at the University of Akron. If SVSM was going to win a third consecutive state title, they'd have to do it without their old coach.

The new SVSM coach was Coach Dru, whom LeBron and the others loved but weren't sure would be as tough on them as Coach Dambrot had been. No matter how good SVSM played, Coach Dambrot found room for improvement and demanded perfection.

"Practice isn't supposed to be fun," Coach Dambrot used to say. "Winning games is fun."

Like it or not, his strategy worked wonders. In LeBron's first two seasons, SVSM had gone 53–1.

"I know [LeBron] hated me," Coach Dambrot said. "I know they all hated me. But I felt I owed them that. They all had so much talent, especially LeBron. I couldn't allow them to coast."

LeBron did, indeed, grow frustrated with Coach Dambrot never letting up during those first two years. They'd win a game by forty and still get yelled at.

"He cussed us out every single practice," LeBron said.

Still, LeBron knew Coach Dambrot was trying to

help, not hurt. He knew Coach Dambrot was trying to make him better.

"Our relationship grew more and more, and he ended up being probably the best coach I ever played for," LeBron said.

Now Coach Dru had to step in and deal with the pressure of trying to go undefeated against a schedule featuring some of the best teams in the country.

By that time, LeBron was such a phenomenon that SVSM's small on-campus gym couldn't handle the crowds that came to watch him play. It felt like everyone in Akron wanted to be at every game. And now basketball fans were driving in from all over Ohio, all over the Midwest even, to catch a live glimpse of the teenage wonder. Even after SVSM moved to James A. Rhodes Arena on the campus of the University of Akron, which seated around fifty-five hundred fans, every game was sold out, with fans slipping in and crowding corners and walkways, willing to stand just to watch LeBron.

The season started okay, with SVSM jumping to a 7–0 record. LeBron was pouring in points and delighting fans. Even though they were winning, the team wasn't quite as sharp as they had been during previous seasons. They soon lost to a team from

New York during a holiday tournament in Delaware. Yet then they managed to peel off eight victories before a huge showdown loomed against Oak Hill Academy.

SVSM had been waiting a year for the rematch. Oak Hill's stars from the previous year had graduated, but a new crop of talented players had arrived from around the country, including a kid from Baltimore named Carmelo Anthony. LeBron had gotten to know Carmelo at various summer camps. He knew the six-foot-eight senior was not just one of the best players he'd ever seen, but a likely NBA superstar in the future as well.

The game was played in Trenton, New Jersey, and attracted an overflowing crowd of around eleven thousand. NBA scouts, college recruiters, and members of the media were everywhere. If anyone could stop LeBron, people figured, it would be Carmelo.

It was a huge event and Carmelo and LeBron didn't disappoint. They put on a show. LeBron scored thirty-six points, grabbed eight rebounds, dished five assists, and made six steals defensively. Carmelo countered with thirty-four points, eleven rebounds, and two assists.

In the end, Oak Hill won 72–66. They were still

too strong for SVSM. It wasn't just Carmelo; they had six other players on that team—all seniors—who would receive Division I college scholarships. Oak Hill would finish the season 32–1 and second in the *USA Today* poll. SVSM was good, but even with LeBron they couldn't climb over Oak Hill and win a national title.

The question was, could they even win a state title?

SVSM entered the state championship game against Roger Bacon High School with a record of 75–0 against Ohio teams since the Fab Four came to the school. Yet in front of an Ohio record crowd of 18,375 fans, Roger Bacon took a big lead early and held off SVSM, 72–66.

"I respect them a lot," LeBron said after the loss, praising his opponent even though he was frustrated with the result.

LeBron would be named Ohio's Mr. Basketball, *USA Today* National Player of the Year, and would finish averaging 28.0 points, 8.9 rebounds, and 6.0 assists. In spite of his personal accomplishments, the loss gnawed at LeBron and his teammates. They were too talented to lose. They thought they should have won the state title all four years they were in high school. Instead they had lost four times that year. They knew if their senior year was going to be different, they had to stop coasting and take every practice and every opponent seriously.

It was the only way, because the circus that had become LeBron-mania was only going to get bigger.

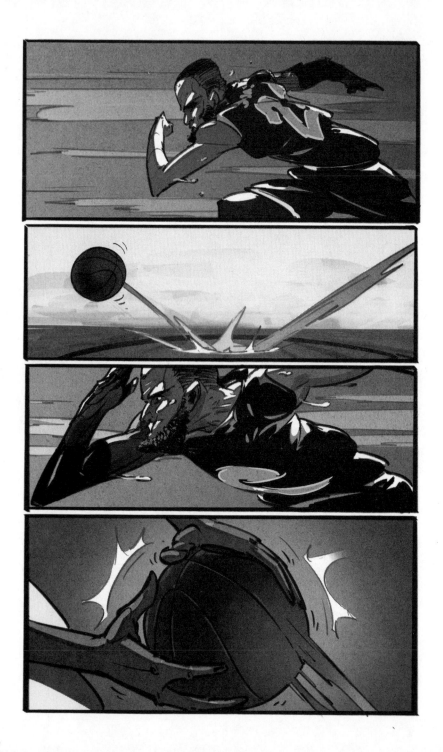

7

Senior Year

BY THE START of his senior year, LeBron James was the most famous high school student in the country. His face was plastered on television practically every day. Basketball fans were obsessed with him. His fame skyrocketed to the point that even non-sports fans wanted a glimpse. He drew a crowd just going out to the mall. Everyone wanted his autograph. SVSM had to ban fellow students from asking LeBron for his signature because it was disrupting class. Teachers were determined to make LeBron's school life as calm and normal as they could.

College coaches gave up offering him scholarships. At the time, the NBA allowed players to enter the draft once they had graduated from high school, so everyone knew that LeBron would skip college altogether and become the number one pick in the 2003 NBA draft.

In the NBA, the team that finishes with the worst record has the best chance to secure the number one overall pick. The nearby Cleveland Cavaliers, LeBron's hometown team, were so intent on drafting him that they essentially tried to lose as many games as possible that season. They even traded away their leading scorer before the season began. It worked. The Cavs went just 17–65 on the season—tied for worst record in the league—and routinely lost by 20 points. Cavs fans actually got upset when they won, thus lowering their chances of getting LeBron.

LeBron and his friends would often travel up to Cavaliers games. They were given a special parking spot, courtside seats, and locker room access. Cleveland wanted him to become comfortable with the franchise in case they were able to draft him.

In fact, LeBron began to receive the red carpet treatment everywhere he went. He and his friends got tickets to concerts and parties. He met Jay-Z.

He met 50 Cent. He even traveled to Chicago and played in some pick-up games with Michael Jordan.

LeBron still played for Adidas-affiliated AAU teams and at Adidas camps. SVSM still wore Adidas gear as part of its deal. It wasn't just Sonny Vaccaro who was working to sign him to an endorsement deal, though. Nike and Reebok were also chasing him. So were pro sports agents who wanted to represent him, financial planners who wanted to invest his future millions, and car and jewelry dealers who wanted LeBron to buy from them when he turned pro. There were all sorts of people who claimed they could help him and his mother out.

The challenge was trying to figure out whom to trust. LeBron knew he would soon be a very wealthy person, a multimillionaire at the age of eighteen. But because high school basketball players can't accept money to play, in the fall of his senior year, he and his mom were still broke and living in apartment 602 of the SpringHill Apartments.

If he had been a teen singer or an actor, or even an inventor, he could have been paid immediately. High school basketball players have to wait, though. It was like knowing he would hit the lottery . . . in six months. Meanwhile, everyone was making money off of him. LeBron noticed that when he auto-graphed a basketball for someone, it would soon appear on eBay for three or four hundred dollars. He didn't receive a penny of that. The guy who got him to sign the basketball made all the money. It didn't seem fair.

The positive side was that LeBron got one more year to still be a kid and play ball with his friends. Determined to stay focused and finish their high school careers out, the now Fab Five (Romeo had become a trusted player) started 3–0. That's when the annual game against Oak Hill arrived, this time bigger than ever.

The game was played at Cleveland State University before a sold-out crowd of over thirteen thousand. More than one hundred journalists and reporters attended, as well as NBA scouts from all over. The game was even broadcast live on ESPN2, giving every fan in the country a chance to watch LeBron and see if he measured up to the hype. ESPN had never before shown a high school basketball game. The anticipation was incredible.

For all the excitement and attention swirling off of the court, for SVSM this was about finally beating Oak Hill. This was the hurdle they hadn't been able to clear and they knew that without beating the best, they couldn't be declared the best. Back in fifth grade, after that first AAU national tournament, they had begun dreaming of bringing a national championship to their hometown. Now they were seniors. This was it, their last chance.

This time felt different, too. LeBron and the guys no longer had any fear of Oak Hill. They respected them, but after the previous two seasons, the Fab Five believed if they played their game, they were unbeatable.

That doesn't mean there weren't some early jitters, especially with TV cameras pointing directly at them. Eventually, though, they took the lead late in the third quarter and refused to be stopped. LeBron had a steal and massive dunk that still gets played on *SportsCenter* and in commercials today. It helped seal the 65–45 victory. He had thirty-one points and thirteen rebounds, and all over America people agreed he was as good as advertised. Around 1.7 million people tuned in to watch.

"He's the best high school player I've ever seen," said Oak Hill's legendary coach, Steve Smith, who had seen just about every great one during his career.

For SVSM, beating Oak Hill felt like a weight had

been taken off their shoulders. The guys jumped around and celebrated at the final buzzer. On the biggest night, with everyone watching, they had proven that Akron could stand strong with anyone in the country.

There was still work to be done, however. SVSM won its next four, setting up another nationally televised game against Mater Dei High School, which is near Los Angeles. Mater Dei was a power in California and featured a number of the same players from the California All-Stars AAU team that had denied the Shooting Stars a national title back in LeBron's eighth-grade year. This was a chance for some long-awaited revenge.

This game was shown on ESPN2 and played at the University of California, Los Angeles's famous Pauley Pavilion. SVSM would no longer be the home team. They were a long way from Akron, playing in front of a frenzied crowd, but SVSM didn't blink. They won 64–58.

The most amazing thing about that victory? LeBron didn't play well, missing all nine of his three-point attempts and scoring "just" twenty-one points. Instead, Romeo and Dru carried the load and everyone played great defense. LeBron wasn't happy with his performance, but he was proud of his friends. He'd been telling everyone since they were kids that he wasn't a one-man team. Now everyone could see it was true.

Both Dru and Romeo had accepted scholarships to play for the University of Akron, where Keith Dambrot was an assistant coach but would soon become the head coach. Willie was headed to play Division II basketball at Fairmont State University in West Virginia. Sian, meanwhile, was headed to Ohio State to play football.

"This team has a lot of good players," Coach Dru said. "They just happen to play in the shadow of the greatest player in Ohio high school basketball history."

With that, SVSM took over as the number one team in America in the *USA Today* poll.

Around that time, Gloria gave LeBron a present for his eighteenth birthday—a brand-new car. It was a Hummer H1, which cost around fifty thousand dollars. Obviously, LeBron's mom didn't have that much money to buy a new car for her son, but the dealer was willing to give her a loan knowing that LeBron would be able to pay for it in just two or three months. LeBron's birthday is in late December. By the end of March, the high school basketball season would be over and LeBron would be free to sign a sneaker contract that would make him incredibly wealthy.

When word got out that LeBron was driving a new, expensive truck, opposing fans and some media began to question if he should still be eligible to play high school basketball. An amateur is not supposed to be compensated for playing and, while Gloria was going to have to pay for the truck eventually, people wondered if getting it early was a violation. The Ohio High School Athletic Association (OHSAA) began investigating, and sports analysts on ESPN and around the country began debating LeBron's truck.

LeBron felt a lot of pressure and a lot of shame that his mother was being criticized for buying him a car even though she didn't have a lot of money. Many parents buy their kids cars. Gloria was upset that she may have gotten LeBron in trouble. It was stressful. LeBron responded by showing up for a game with a remote-controlled toy Hummer, driving it around the court as television cameras filmed it, and then scoring a school-record-breaking fifty points in the victory. He was determined not to let the incident bother him. Meanwhile, the OHSAA eventually decided Gloria had gotten the loan on her own and cleared LeBron.

Unfortunately, the investigations weren't done. Soon after the Hummer controversy, LeBron and some friends were at a local mall. They walked into a store and LeBron began looking at a couple of throwback sports jerseys. They were each worth around $845. The owner told LeBron he could have them as a gift because he had read in the newspaper that LeBron had made the honor roll. A thankful LeBron then posed for a picture with the store owner, who hung it on the wall.

When the OHSAA found out, it ruled that Le-Bron received the jerseys in exchange for the picture, which could be seen as an advertisement for the store. They then suspended LeBron for the rest of the season. "This is a direct violation of the OHSAA bylaws on amateurism because, in fact, LeBron did capitalize on athletic fame by receiving these gifts," the OHSAA said.

LeBron was crushed. He didn't mean to violate any bylaws. He didn't want to be suspended for the season. He was a kid who wanted the jerseys and thought they were a gift. He quickly returned the jerseys, but the damage was done.

"If I had known I was violating anything, I never would have done it," LeBron told CBS News. "I would have never jeopardized my eligibility. I would have never jeopardized my team."

If he wanted to make money off of his fame or his basketball talent, he could have made millions and just skipped his senior season, signed a deal with Adidas or Nike, and trained on the side for the NBA draft. The reason he didn't was because he wanted to enjoy his final year of high school basketball and win the state and national titles with his friends.

Besides, he had made just about everyone around him a lot of money. That included the OHSAA, which ran the state tournament and sold out every arena he played in. A huge national debate broke out about whether LeBron deserved the suspension, with many fans and media siding with LeBron.

"It's ridiculous to do this to the kid," Shaquille O'Neal, then of the Los Angeles Lakers and, at the time, one of the biggest stars in the NBA, told the *New York Times*. "Everybody's capitalizing on him. And you guys try to persecute his character and take away his high school career over two jerseys?"

For LeBron, the worst part was that the OHSAA determined that since he had received the gifts prior to SVSM's most recent game, a victory over Buchtel, LeBron was actually retroactively ineligible to play in that game. As such, SVSM had to forfeit the game. They were now 13–1, no longer undefeated. The national title felt lost.

Gloria and LeBron hired a lawyer and began to fight the suspension. Meanwhile, LeBron had to sit out a game against Canton's McKinley Senior High School. He served as an assistant coach and rooted for his teammates from the bench. They managed to win, 63–62. How long could they keep it up without their leader, though?

Days later, LeBron received good news. A judge ruled in his favor and said LeBron could play while the courts sorted out whether or not the OHSAA could suspend him for the season. He still might be suspended, but in the meantime, he could at least play. It was just in time for a big game against Los Angeles's Westchester High School. Other than the state final, this was the toughest game left on the schedule. Westchester was ranked seventh by *USA Today*.

LeBron had a great deal of frustration to unleash.

With over eight thousand fans in attendance in an arena in New Jersey, including the usual array of scouts and media from around the country watching his every move, LeBron came out and drained his first three shots. Then he started whipping perfect passes across the court. Then he scored some more. During one stretch, he poured in eighteen consecutive points. Westchester had a number of future college players on the roster, but it stood no chance against LeBron. The final score was 78–52 SVSM and LeBron alone scored fifty-two points, nearly outscoring Westchester all by himself.

"We could have put three guys on him and he would have hit those shots," Westchester's coach, Ed Azzam, said.

Victory aside, the ongoing battle over LeBron's high school eligibility had become a major national news story, with nightly updates on ESPN, CBS, NBC, and ABC. Reporters constantly hung around Akron, covering not just every SVSM game, but even its practices. The Fighting Irish just wanted the circus to end.

Finally, a ruling came: The OHSAA would not suspend LeBron for the rest of the season, but he would be given a two-game suspension. Since he already sat out one game, he'd only have to miss one more and the matter would be done.

SVSM decided the game for LeBron to miss would be the season finale against a team from Toledo. When a snowstorm prevented them from traveling to Akron, a local high school, Firestone, filled in. Even without LeBron, this was a mismatch. SVSM won big, 90–43.

The school held a ceremony after the game and retired LeBron's number 23 jersey. The crowd cheered. Coach Dru gave a speech. LeBron was overjoyed by the support his school, his community, and his friends had given him even when things got tough and it felt like everyone was against him. He had arrived not knowing what to expect, or even if he should trust the people at St. Vincent-St. Mary. He was leaving a hero who had found a home.

"It's unimaginable," LeBron said that night. "It's not just all me, I feel like my teammates were a part of that, too. On the other side of that jersey, it should say 'teammates,' because they helped me get to this point."

Part of his excitement was that *USA Today* still ranked SVSM number one in the country, despite officially having one loss. The newspaper decided the forfeited game was meaningless. Now SVSM just had to finish the job.

It rolled through the state playoffs, reaching the finals against Kettering's Archbishop Alter High School. The Irish had previously blown Alter out by thirty-three points back in February, so this time Alter tried to hold the ball when they got possession and slow the game down to keep it close. It worked, sort of. The final score was just 40–36, but SVSM won. LeBron had twenty-five points.

The Fab Five didn't care about the margin of victory. They hugged and waved their index fingers in the air to signal they were number one. They posed for pictures with the trophy. They celebrated with their parents and classmates. They thanked Coach Dru for all he had done and how he had always believed in them, all the way back to grade school.

They had won a third state title in four years. LeBron was named Mr. Basketball for a third time after averaging 30.4 points and 9.7 rebounds for the season. Most importantly, they were declared national champions. The Akron kids had finally done it and put their city on the map. And they had done it together. They grew up together. Matured together. Laughed together. Learned together. And won together.

"Our friendship is beyond anything I've ever been a part of," LeBron said years later. "We've been best friends since we were nine years old."

And now, for LeBron, it was time to head to the NBA.

8

NBA Life

THE CLEVELAND CAVALIERS' strategy of losing as many games as possible so they could draft LeBron James worked. The Cavs got the first pick in the 2003 NBA draft, and there was never a doubt whom they would select—the high school sensation from their backyard of Akron. The moment the Cavs were granted the first pick, the phones in their ticket office began ringing and ringing with fans looking to buy season tickets.

Before the draft even arrived, though, LeBron had some other business to handle. Finally allowed to cash in on his ability and fame, he had a number of endorsement deals to sign. The biggest was choosing a shoe company. He had worn Adidas throughout high school and enjoyed a friendship with Sonny Vaccaro. Nike and Reebok were also offering a lot of money and the opportunity to create his own line of basketball sneakers. LeBron picked Nike, which was the shoe company of his idol, Michael Jordan, in part because it offered the most money, an astounding ninety million dollars paid over seven years. It was the biggest endorsement deal ever handed out to an NBA rookie.

Instantly, LeBron was financially set for life, even if he somehow never played a single NBA game.

With his future secure, LeBron set his sights on his new team. There were plenty of positives to becoming a Cavalier. Cleveland was familiar for LeBron. He knew the team, the players, and the coaches. He knew the media in Northeast Ohio. He could buy a house on the north side of Akron and commute up for games. His mom would be nearby. Many of his friends would be around also, including his old teammate Maverick Carter, who was finishing up a business degree at the University of Akron.

There was a downside, though. The Cavs were

terrible. Their pitiful 17–65 record marked their fifth consecutive losing season. As a franchise, not only had they never won the NBA title, they had never even reached the NBA Finals. They rarely had any good players. LeBron had gone 101–6 at St. Vincent-St. Mary, and one of those losses was a forfeit. He wasn't used to losing. As good as he was projected to be, he was still just an eighteen-year-old rookie surrounded by bad NBA players.

LeBron's first NBA game was in Sacramento against the Kings on October 29, 2003. Even though it was a road game, his presence created a sensation. The arena was sold out. A nearby mall reported running out of number 23 Cleveland jerseys, the number LeBron would wear to follow in the footsteps of Michael Jordan. It became an international spectacle, with basketball fans all over the world wanting to see LeBron in action.

But perhaps the most excited person of all was LeBron himself, who'd achieved his lifelong goal of making the NBA. "I'm finally here," he said. "It's a dream."

Early in the game he threw a pass to a teammate for a perfect alley-oop dunk. Then he hit his first three jump shots. The crowd was rooting for the

Kings, of course, but there was excitement every time LeBron got the ball. He scored twenty-five points, grabbed six rebounds, dished nine assists, and made four steals. Despite his amazing debut, Cleveland lost, 106–92.

It was a preview of the season ahead—LeBron continued to mesmerize fans, but his teammates couldn't keep up. In his first year, LeBron proved he belonged despite arriving with no college basketball experience. He averaged 20.9 points a game and scored over thirty points thirteen times and even recorded forty-one once. While there were other days he struggled shooting and scoring against great NBA defenders, there was no doubting his potential. He was named the NBA Rookie of the Year. Cleveland went just 35–47 and missed the playoffs, though.

That summer, LeBron was named to the United States Men's National Basketball Team and competed in the Olympics in Athens, Greece. It was his first Olympics and another dream come true. He was used mostly as a reserve and the team did not fare as well as expected, capturing a bronze medal, just the third time it hadn't won gold.

In his second year in the NBA, 2004–05, both LeBron and the Cavs were better. LeBron averaged

27.2 points a game and Cleveland went 42–40, its first winning record in seven years, although they failed to reach the playoffs. LeBron did get selected to his first All-Star game, at just twenty years old, trailing only Kobe Bryant as the youngest ever to accomplish the feat. He was also named second team All-NBA, signifying he was already one of the ten best players in the league.

Top ten was impressive, but LeBron's unstoppable work ethic, drilled into him by his past coaches, made him strive to be the best. He spent his summers working on his jump shot to become a more complete scorer. He also watched endless game film, trying to figure out how he could continue to get his teammates more involved in the action. He knew the Cavs couldn't be a one-man team.

"Individual accolades," LeBron said, "it doesn't mean anything to me. I've always felt when the team is successful, individual accolades always come."

The 2005–06 Cavs began to come into their own. They started the season 9–2, with LeBron leading the way. Cleveland had built a decent team around him with some good defensive players and jump shooters. Mostly, though, they played hard. LeBron was determined to win games and, despite being still so young, he was the leader. He averaged 31.4 points a game that year, the highest for a single season in his career (as of 2019), and twice put up more than fifty points in a game. He was named first team All-NBA and came in second in voting for the MVP, trailing only Steve Nash of the Phoenix Suns.

The Cleveland roster was young and exciting, and LeBron was one of the most popular players in the league. The Cavs went 50–32, enough to reach the playoffs for the first time in seven seasons. Very few people around the NBA or in the media thought they'd make much of an impact in the playoffs, but LeBron was determined to show the team was for real.

They managed to do that by beating the Washington Wizards in the first round of the playoffs, four games to two. LeBron was incredible, averaging an astounding 35.7 points a game in the series, including scoring 45 points and hitting the game winner with 0.9 seconds left in the critical Game 5. Everyone in basketball had spoken about LeBron's future since he was a high school star in Akron. It was clear that the future had arrived. LeBron was a force to be reckoned with.

The problem for the Cavs was their second-round opponent—the Detroit Pistons. Detroit had won the 2004 NBA Championship and returned to The

Finals in 2005 before losing in seven games to the San Antonio Spurs. They were a veteran team that played tremendous defense and were determined to win the title again. Cleveland, on the other hand, was a young team with a young big-name star that hadn't proved itself yet. The Pistons were not going to be intimidated.

It showed in the first two games: Detroit won them both, including a twenty-seven-point blowout in Game 1. The team's strategy was to bang and hit LeBron as often as possible, figuring the refs wouldn't call a foul every time. LeBron still played well, scoring twenty-two and thirty respectively in the first two games, but with all the defensive pressure, his efforts fell short.

In Game 3, however, Cleveland roared back and won. LeBron played all forty-eight minutes and finished with a triple-double: twenty-one points, ten rebounds, and ten assists. The Pistons were not pleased. They expected to make quick work of the Cavs. One of their star players, Rasheed Wallace, publicly guaranteed that Detroit would win Game 4. Cleveland took it as extra motivation, winning 74–72 to tie the series and making Wallace eat his words.

"We're not feeling any pressure," LeBron said. "The Pistons are."

Wallace was undeterred and made another guarantee, promising Detroit wouldn't lose the series. Then came Game 5, back in Detroit, and Cleveland won again, behind LeBron's thirty-two points, to take a 3–2 lead in the series.

These young upstarts were on the verge of shocking the veteran Pistons right out of the playoffs. That's when Detroit showed why they were a championship team.

"We don't panic," said star center Ben Wallace. Detroit rallied to win the next two matchups and advance to the Eastern Conference Finals. Just like that, Cleveland saw its season fall apart.

LeBron got his first lesson in how intense playoff basketball was. The Cavs lacked the experience and talent to close out the series, but that didn't mean the twenty-one-year-old hadn't served notice to the NBA.

"There's nobody on his level that can get his teammates involved like he does," Detroit's Tayshaun Prince said. "He sees the plays before they even happen, and no one else does that."

For LeBron, getting a taste of playoff basketball helped him focus even more on raising his game. As much as the NBA is always competitive, it ramps up in the playoffs. It gets more physical. It gets more emotional. Every possession matters. A team has to make the most of every opportunity. He loved it. He wanted more of it.

Technically, LeBron could have still been a college kid, about to enter his senior year. Most people that age are still trying to figure out what career they want to pursue. But since high school, LeBron had needed to grow up faster than those around him, and he developed into an adult while others his age were still figuring out their lives. He moved into a large home outside of Akron. He lived there with his girlfriend and future wife, Savannah Brinson.

Savannah had grown up on the west side of Akron, just like LeBron. She was one year younger than him and attended Buchtel High School. One day, LeBron spotted her while at a football game. He asked a mutual friend for her number, but she refused and took his instead. When she eventually reached out, he invited her to an SVSM basketball game.

"I went, and I was like, 'Wow, this guy is pretty popular in here,'" Savannah later told *Harper's Bazaar*.

After the game, LeBron, Savannah, and a group

of friends went to Applebee's. Later LeBron asked her out and took her to Outback Steakhouse on their first date. They have been together ever since. In 2004, they had a son together, LeBron James Jr., who is called "Bronny." He was the first of three children—Bryce was born in 2007, and Zhuri was born in 2014.

In May of 2007, LeBron and the Cavs were back in the same position, trailing a very confident Detroit team 2–0 in the playoffs. This time it was the Eastern Conference Finals, with a trip to the NBA Finals on the line. Cleveland had won fifty games again, and then defeated both Washington and New Jersey to earn a rematch with the veteran Pistons. Whereas Oak Hill had once been the thorn in LeBron's side, now Detroit filled that role. LeBron knew that until he could get past these guys, he couldn't truly thrive.

In the first two games, Detroit again bullied and banged on LeBron, limiting his scoring and leaving most of the NBA to assume that the Cavs still weren't ready to play with the best in the league. Many criticized LeBron, saying he wasn't aggressive enough and passed too often. They said he needed to shoot more.

Then the Cavs returned to Cleveland for Games 3 and 4 and LeBron began to figure out how to beat the tough Detroit defense. He scored thirty-two and Cleveland won Game 3. He scored twenty-five and Cleveland won Game 4. Then came a huge Game 5 back in Detroit. With 2:17 remaining in the fourth quarter, the Pistons led 88–84. The crowd at the Palace of Auburn Hills was roaring with delight, expecting a Detroit victory that would push the Cavs to the brink. They could sense the Pistons were destined to return to The Finals and that Cleveland would again be proven to be pretenders.

That's when LeBron decided that he was going to do whatever it took to win this game. He drained a three-point shot. Then he had a dunk. Then, trailing by two with just 9.1 seconds left, he drove to the lane and dunked again to tie it at 91 and force a five-minute overtime.

The plan for the Cavs was now simple. Let LeBron hold the ball at the top of the key and get all the other players out of the way. From there, he could either drive to the basket, pull up, and shoot, or, if needed, pass it off to an open teammate. Mostly LeBron did the shooting, scoring nine points on a dunk, a jumper, and five free throws. Meanwhile everyone else played defense. LeBron did, too. At the end of the first overtime, the score was 100–100. Time for a second overtime!

It was more of the same. LeBron hit three jumpers, including a three-pointer. Detroit tried everything to stop him. They put different defenders on him. They double-teamed him. They sought to confuse him. "We tried to trap him and get it out of his hands," Pistons coach Flip Saunders said. It didn't work.

Finally, with the game tied 107–107 and just 11.4 seconds remaining, LeBron got the ball. Detroit put its best player, Chauncey Billups, on him, and also had all four of its other defenders watching closely. LeBron took Chauncey off the dribble to the left, then blew past him as the four other Pistons collapsed toward the hoop. LeBron leaped and slipped right between all of them before scooping a layup off the glass and through the basket.

Cleveland 109, Detroit 107. The Cavs won. It was an astounding shot that capped off an astonishing performance. LeBron scored the final twenty-five points and twenty-nine of the Cavs' final thirty points of the game. Let that sink in: No other Cleveland player recorded a point from late in the fourth quarter through either overtime. He totaled forty-eight points, plus nine rebounds, and seven assists. It was a performance like no one had imagined possible.

"I've never seen anybody dominate a game like that, especially considering the situation, Eastern Conference Finals, on the road, against a very good defensive team," Cavs center Zydrunas Ilgauskas marveled.

LeBron said he was "exhausted." And not satisfied. Taking a 3–2 lead wasn't the ultimate goal. Winning the series was. The Pistons were now rattled, though, and Cleveland closed out the series 98–82. In just his fourth season, at age twenty-two, LeBron was going to The Finals to play for the NBA title.

"If I could put into words what's going on in my head right now, man, we would be up here for another three hours," LeBron said. "But this is special, the guys were really mentally prepared. I never put a time limit on when I thought we could reach this point."

Beating the Pistons had meant a lot to LeBron. "They helped me out with my development," LeBron said. "It worked my mental toughness, my physical toughness, just my competitive nature. Just in understanding what you need in order to be successful, how to win and how to compete."

The Cavs' biggest obstacle, the San Antonio Spurs, was poised to teach LeBron another lesson in The Finals. The Spurs were led by three incredible players—Tim Duncan, Manu Ginobili, and Tony Parker—who will surely be Hall of Famers in the future. They were coached by another sure-bet future Hall of Famer, Gregg Popovich. They were in The Finals seeking their fourth NBA Championship in nine seasons.

They were too talented and too experienced for the Cavs to handle. The Spurs had so many good players that they could rotate defenders on LeBron, and if one player had an off night, there was someone else capable of stepping up. They bottled up LeBron, who averaged just 22.0 points a night and shot 35.6 percent from the field. The Spurs swept the series, 4–0, to win the title. LeBron was disappointed, but marveled at the quality of San Antonio's play and vowed to one day be on a team like that.

"They don't have the greatest athletes in the world, they don't have the greatest shooters in the world, but they have probably the greatest team in the world, and that's what this sport is all about," LeBron said. "It's not about an individual. It's not like tennis, it's not like golf."

Despite the loss, LeBron's magical ride to The Finals, years before anyone thought he'd be able to do it, impressed everyone. After the series was over, Tim Duncan hugged LeBron and tried to offer some encouragement.

"This is going to be your league in a little while."

9

The Decision

THERE ARE THIRTY TEAMS in the NBA, but there can only be one champion. Forming a championship-caliber team is about more than finding the perfect collection of talent—you also need players who truly want to sacrifice for the team. Teams that win it all have a special, cohesive group; it's not enough to just have the best player. They need the entire team and a coach working together. Some of the greatest players in NBA history have never won a title.

As much as Cleveland had taken a step toward a

championship, they still had a long way to go. Getting swept by San Antonio proved that. So did the 2007–08 season that followed.

LeBron averaged 30.0 points a game, was named the All-Star game MVP for the second time, and earned first team All-NBA honors, but there weren't enough good players around him. After winning fifty games in each of the two previous seasons, Cleveland regressed and won just forty-five. The Cavs reached the playoffs but lost to the Boston Celtics, 4–3, in the second round. LeBron scored forty-five points in the decisive Game 7, but it wasn't enough. Boston had four great players—Kevin Garnett, Paul Pierce, Ray Allen, and Rajon Rondo, plus a bunch of role players. Not even LeBron could take them all on.

Privately, LeBron was growing frustrated that Cleveland hadn't surrounded him with other great players. Both San Antonio and Boston had multiple All-Stars and future Hall of Famers. As much as he loved his teammates, no one else was an elite player. Until that changed, the season was going to end in defeat, not the championship he coveted.

That summer, Cleveland made a big trade, getting guard Mo Williams, who was an excellent scorer. In games when LeBron's shot wasn't falling, Mo could step in and Cleveland could still win. He became an All-Star in 2008–09, scoring over forty twice and over thirty on five occasions. That helped LeBron play better than ever also—he averaged 28.4 points a game. He also had three different fifty-plus-point nights.

That season LeBron was named the league's Most Valuable Player for the first time. He won 96.7 percent of the votes, a landslide victory over the Los Angeles Lakers' Kobe Bryant. At twenty-four, LeBron was undeniably the best basketball player in the world. When he was informed that he won, he told the NBA he didn't want the ceremony to be held at the Cavs' home arena in Cleveland, as would usually be the case. He had another location that meant more to him . . . Akron.

"This is a place where all my dreams started and where I thought they could become real," LeBron said. "There's really not a better place."

The old St. Vincent-St. Mary gym was packed as LeBron accepted the award. His Cavs teammates were there. His coaches. His childhood friends. Sian Cotton came, although the rest of Fab Five were out of town. Coach Dru was there, and LeBron made sure to thank the man who had believed so deeply in him.

"I may not have had a biological father around every day . . . but that man right there helped me do a lot of things that my father would have helped me with," LeBron said. Pam and Frank Walker, and all their kids, were also in attendance. LeBron honored them by saying, "the Walker family was instrumental to why I am up here."

And he spent a good deal of time talking about his mother, who was sitting in the front row. When he drove to the ceremony, he made sure to pass by some of his old Akron spots: the many houses where he was raised, the memory-filled playgrounds where he and his friends first played the game for fun, and the SpringHill apartment, where he finally had his own room and could think about what he might accomplish.

"Growing up, for her to be a single parent . . . [with] no father figure around, no father to help raise a young man like myself, I tell Savannah, there is no way, even in the [financial] position I am today, there is no way I could raise LeBron [Jr.] or Bryce by myself . . . I don't know how you did it . . . I may be able to figure how to hit a jumper or dunk the basketball, but I cannot figure out how you did it by yourself. Wow."

Mostly, though, he wanted to inspire the kids of Akron and beyond. And not just by giving back—he donated the new car he received as part of winning the award to charity—but more importantly, by encouraging all the people living in smaller cities or rural communities where you are often told that you can't be as good as someone from a large community. He encouraged them to believe they could transcend limits others place on you. He encouraged them to dream big.

He recalled how as a kid he'd tell people he wanted to one day become the MVP of the NBA. "They'd say, 'Who do you think you are? You're from Akron,'" LeBron said. "You never think something like this is going to happen growing up in the city of Akron. You look on TV and hear about cities like Chicago and Los Angeles and New York City. You never think someone from Akron, Ohio, will do the things we did growing up."

The MVP award was great, but LeBron repeatedly said it meant nothing compared to team accomplishments. Above all, he wanted a championship parade in downtown Cleveland.

Hopes were high. The Cavs had started the 2008–09 season 26–4 and finished with the best record in the league, 66–16. No Cavalier team had ever won more games. As the wins piled up, Cleveland fans began to believe that they were cheering for the best team in the league and the city's long championship drought was about to end.

Cleveland entered the playoffs as the favorite to win the championship and promptly swept their first two opponents. Then came the Eastern Conference Finals against the Orlando Magic and their seven-foot center, Dwight Howard. The Magic shocked the Cavaliers in the first game in Cleveland. In Game 2, the teams were tied at 95 when Orlando's Hedo Turkoglu hit a jumper with 1.0 second left to give the Magic a two-point lead and what seemed like a certain victory.

The Cavs called a time-out. They were desperate to win and avoid going behind 2–0 in the series. Could they even set up and execute a shot in only one second?

On the inbound, they passed the ball to LeBron. He caught it at the top of the key, twenty-five feet from the basket, behind the three-point line. There was no time to do anything but rise up and shoot, even though he was closely guarded. As he let it go and the ball sailed to the basket, the entire arena in Cleveland held their breath. This was as close to silent as twenty thousand fans could be. The only noise was the final buzzer sounding as the shot flew through the air. If it went in, Cleveland won. If not, Cleveland lost.

It went in. The arena exploded with noise. "You couldn't hear anything but just a roar," LeBron said. His teammates mobbed him for hitting one of the most dramatic game-winning shots in NBA history. "It's the biggest shot I have made in my career," LeBron said.

While that win tied the series at 1–1, it did nothing to stop Orlando's growing confidence. The Magic had a number of great players and won three of the next four games to take the series. In Game 6, Dwight Howard scored forty points and grabbed fourteen rebounds to eliminate the Cavs and end what once looked like a dream season for them.

The loss was devastating for LeBron. He had been statistically brilliant, doing just about everything possible—averaging 38.5 points, 8.3 rebounds, and 8.0 assists in the series. And his teammates had played about as well as they were capable. Yet they still weren't good enough to even return to the NBA Finals, let alone win it all (Los Angeles would defeat Orlando for the title).

LeBron began to wonder if he could ever win a championship in Cleveland. He loved and supported his town and teammates, but he felt no closer to a title. He knew after the 2009–10 season, he would be a free agent and could sign with any team in the NBA. It was difficult to even imagine him leaving his beloved Northeast Ohio. LeBron had always dreamed of winning an NBA title for Cleveland. How could he give up on that goal, fans wondered? But LeBron couldn't just think of the fans or the city anymore—he was determined to do what was best for him and his family as well.

The 2009–10 season played out much like the last one. LeBron was the overwhelming choice for NBA MVP. He averaged 29.7 points, 7.3 rebounds, and 8.6 assists a game. He did everything he could to lift his teammates up. Cleveland won an impressive sixty-one games. It entered the playoffs as a favorite again. Then in the second round, the Cavs ran into Boston and their four star players.

The Celtics were too much. One game it was Kevin Garnett leading the way. The next it was Ray Allen or Rajon Rondo or Paul Pierce. Boston won the series 4–2. It didn't have the best player, but it certainly had the best team.

As LeBron walked off the court after losing the series in Boston, he took off his Cavs jersey. Fans worried that it might be the last time he ever wore the Cavs' colors.

LeBron was now a free agent and just about everyone wanted him. LeBron and his management team, which now included his old friend Maverick Carter, arranged meetings with the New York Knicks, New Jersey Nets, Chicago Bulls, Miami Heat, Los Angeles Clippers, and, of course, the Cavs. Each team laid out impressive plans on how they would use him as a player and how they would build a championship team around him.

The secret weapon, though, was one of LeBron's good friends and fellow NBA star, Dwyane Wade. He was drafted the same year as LeBron and played for the Miami Heat. He had already won the NBA championship in 2006 with the Heat. The two had become very close playing for USA Basketball at World Championships and the Olympics, where they captured the gold medal in 2008 (they'd go on to win another gold in 2012).

As LeBron considered his options, Dwyane was calling and texting LeBron, telling him to come to

Miami and team up with him and another free agent, former Toronto Raptors big-man Chris Bosh, who had just signed with Miami. Like Dwyane and LeBron, Chris had also been on the Olympic team and was drafted in 2003—LeBron went first overall, Dwyane was picked fourth, and Chris fifth.

Finally, LeBron would be surrounded by other star players. Even better, he knew and trusted Dwyane and Chris. And when Miami gave their presentation, they stressed the bond the team had. It reminded him of the brotherhood he'd felt at SVSM.

"The best part of the meeting was the whole family thing," LeBron said. "[Miami said] 'we are a close-knit family. We do everything as a family. We win. We lose. Blood, sweat, and tears, all that as a family.' And that's what I've always been a part of my whole life. That's always, since I was a kid, what I always [sought]. And when I heard that . . . that was kind of like the icing on the cake for me."

That was enough for LeBron to make the most difficult choice of his life. In a nationally televised announcement dubbed "The Decision," he said he was going to leave his hometown and "take my talents to South Beach," referencing Miami's most famous waterfront area.

"I feel like this is going to give me the best op-portunity to win and win for multiple years," LeBron explained. "And not only to win in the regular sea-son . . . I want to win championships."

The Decision sent shock waves throughout the NBA. Miami was now a league power. Cleveland was doomed without their star. Some fans around the country were upset that star players were teaming up to win, rather than remaining loyal to their original franchises and cities. LeBron thought it was the only way to accomplish his goal, though. He had given Cleveland seven years and it hadn't worked.

Back in Ohio, the news enraged Cavaliers fans, who now considered LeBron a traitor who had abandoned them before delivering a long-awaited championship. They were soon on social media and the local news burning LeBron jerseys and shout-ing insults at him. LeBron saw the images and was hurt. He felt he had done all he could for the fans in Cleveland and Akron, not just on the court but with all his charity work as well.

"I never wanted to leave Cleveland," LeBron said. "And my heart will always be around that area."

There was no turning back now, though. He was taking those talents to South Beach.

10

Champion

MIAMI WAS A FRESH START for LeBron. He was surrounded by his friends . . . who also happened to be incredibly talented players. His family became friends with their families, especially his son Bronny and Dwyane Wade Jr., who were the same age.

There was an incredible pressure to win, however. The Heat were a very serious organization, led by team president Pat Riley, who had won an NBA title as a player with the Knicks, and five of them as a head coach with the Lakers and the Heat. He knew how to build championship teams. It started with demanding the most out of his players. There was no question Miami had enough talent to win it all. With the "Big Three," as LeBron, Dwyane, and Chris had become known, leading the way, anything less than a championship, even a loss in The Finals, would allow critics to rip them apart for failing.

LeBron didn't make it any easier on them when at a fan rally to introduce the signing of him and Chris, he stated he didn't come to Miami to win just one championship, but a lot of them.

"Not two, not three, not four, not five, not six, not seven," LeBron said. "When I say that, I really believe it. I'm about business."

Around the NBA, the one thing the fans of other teams could agree on was that they wanted someone, anyone, other than the Heat to win the 2010–11 NBA Championship. LeBron, and all of Miami, were suddenly NBA villains.

"Being booed, I thrive on it," LeBron said, trying to turn a negative into a positive. "I love it, and you get an opportunity to go into hostile buildings and hear a lot of boos, but at the same time, they respect what you do."

That first regular season was about learning how to deal with those boos and play with each other.

LeBron, Dwyane, and Chris were all used to being the main star on their teams. Now they had to share that role even though they played different positions.

LeBron was a six-foot-eight, two-hundred-and-forty-pound forward who could also bring the ball up like a point guard. He was equally good at shooting three-pointers, driving to the rim, and grabbing rebounds against other big men. Dwyane was a six-foot-five guard who used his athletic ability and speed to slice through defenses. And Chris was a six-foot-eleven forward who, despite being so tall, could shoot from deep, where his shot was almost impossible to block.

After a disappointing start to the regular season, the team worked out the early kinks and started to find their rhythm. The Heat went 58–24, a good season by any standard. They then stormed through the first three rounds of the playoffs, beating Philadelphia, Boston, and Chicago each 4 games to 1. The team was beginning to jell, with the guys taking turns exploiting other defenses. LeBron, Dwyane, and Chris were each leading scorers for the Heat in multiple games during those series. Miami's plan was working perfectly.

The Dallas Mavericks were waiting in The Finals.

While Miami was heavily favored, Dallas presented a difficult matchup. Their star was Dirk Nowitzki, a seven-footer from Germany, who was one of the best in the game and broke the standard mold of a big man with his incredible outside shooting ability. But mostly Dallas had a team that worked well together, getting the most out of each player's talent. Miami would have to play its best.

The Heat started the series up 2–1, but Dallas buckled down and took control. Nowitzki was tough to stop and LeBron began to struggle with his outside shooting. He'd averaged just 17.8 points in The Finals, way below normal. He missed repeatedly with the game on the line, while Nowitzki hit key shot after key shot. It allowed LeBron's critics again to question whether he was mentally strong enough, or clutch enough, to win an NBA title like the true greats of the game.

LeBron heard that, but he couldn't prove them wrong. Dallas won the last three games of the series, celebrating their championship on Miami's home court.

The Heat, especially LeBron, Dwyane, and Chris, were stunned. They had come together to win championships, not fall short. LeBron congratulated the

Mavs but walked off the court with his head down. Chris appeared to weep. This was part frustration, part humiliation. They had put a target on their backs by coming together and promising such lofty goals. Then they failed.

"There's definitely a personal failure," LeBron said after. "It hurts me, and I get on myself when I'm not able to play well and help my teammates win."

LeBron was so depressed he went back home and didn't leave his house for two weeks, he later told *Sports Illustrated*. He was embarrassed to be seen in public. He couldn't go on the Internet, check social media, or watch TV because it felt like everyone was laughing at him, picking on him. "Every channel—doesn't matter if it was the Cartoon Channel—was talking about me and the Heat," LeBron later joked.

Here he was, the best basketball player in the world, rich and famous beyond belief, starring in commercials and considering roles in movies, capable of doing anything he wanted . . . except winning a championship. He was miserable.

He flew home to Akron, where he still had a house. For relaxation and exercise, LeBron has always liked to mountain bike. He feels free off in the woods, pedaling a bike and wearing a helmet, where he can be alone with his thoughts. There is no one there to watch him or ask for autographs or critique his game. Some days that summer he would ride seventy miles or more. It helped him get over his frustration.

As for basketball, he called one of his oldest coaches, Coach Dambrot, who was by then the head coach at the University of Akron. Coach Dambrot closed the gym and worked out with LeBron alone, forcefully telling him not how great he was, but how he still had to improve more, how he had to find ways to make his teammates better. More rebounds. More assists. It was like they were back in the old days, when LeBron was just a hopeful kid.

"LeBron has always been willing to listen to instruction and coaching if he trusts you," Dambrot said. "He always wants to get better."

Soon LeBron was no longer feeling sorry for himself. He was just determined to never let the 2010–11 season happen again. There was another thing he had to deal with also. LeBron was never comfortable being the villain. While he tried to brush off having fans boo him and claim it was a sign of respect, in truth he wanted to be liked. He knew that he was at his best when he was enjoying the game and celebrating the fun of basketball. That wasn't the case in Miami.

During the 2011–12 season, there was a noticeable change in LeBron on the court; he tried to smile more. He celebrated less after making a big play, so as not to anger opposing fans. He became comfortable in his own skin and decided that he would just try to be the best version of himself. Whatever everyone was saying about him truly didn't matter. He would be the person he knew he was, take it or leave it.

At the All-Star game that year, he noted, "I'm on the right path, back to playing basketball how I play, and that's having fun at a high level."

LeBron would win his third MVP that year and the Heat roared into the playoffs again as favorites to win the title. The pressure was still there to make good on his championship guarantee. The team felt different, though, and it had added some critical pieces, outside shooters and do-it-all team guys such as Mike Miller and Shane Battier. It wasn't just three All-Stars anymore. It was a team.

They easily advanced to the Eastern Conference Finals, where old foe Boston was waiting. The Celtics still had their slew of All-Stars and they desperately wanted to stop Miami. The Celtics took a 3–2 lead in the series, with Game 6 scheduled in Boston, one of the most challenging and intimidating places to play in the league. This was a chance to end Miami's season even before The Finals. Again, everyone wondered about LeBron's championship-winning ability.

Instead of getting nervous and tense and forcing things, LeBron exhaled and just played his game. He scored fourteen points in the first quarter, giving Miami a ten-point lead and quieting the rowdy crowd. He had sixteen more in the second quarter. Everything LeBron did seemed to work. The Celtics couldn't keep up. The Heat cruised to victory, with LeBron scoring an amazing forty-five points and grabbing fifteen rebounds to force a Game 7.

It was one of the greatest games in NBA history. It was proof to LeBron that his new approach worked.

"I was very immature [last year]," LeBron said. "I played to prove people wrong instead of just playing my game, instead of just going out and having fun and playing a game that I grew up loving."

Two days later, Miami won Game 7 handily, 101–88, with LeBron scoring thirty-one points and twelve rebounds. Getting past Boston felt like a weight had been lifted off Miami's shoulders. They'd stared down defeat and survived.

In The Finals, they would face an Oklahoma team that had three young superstars: Kevin Durant, Russell Westbrook, and James Harden. Their talent was undeniable. They were inexperienced, though. Durant and Westbrook were twenty-four. Harden was only twenty-three. It was a little like when LeBron first made The Finals at age twenty-two. They had ability, but not necessarily the knowledge of how to win a championship.

The Heat were confident. Then Oklahoma City won the first game, 105–94. Miami had the lead for much of it, but OKC was better in the fourth. LeBron had thirty, but didn't score enough late. Suddenly, all the same fears came back. Why couldn't LeBron become a champion? Were the critics right about him?

The Heat refused to panic. They took an early lead in Game 2 and held OKC off late. LeBron scored thirty-two. They built a big second-half lead to win Game 3. LeBron had nineteen points and fourteen rebounds. In Game 4, they staged a comeback to win again. LeBron had twenty-nine points, nine rebounds, and twelve assists despite battling leg cramps. He was playing incredible basketball. The Heat were one game away from winning the championship.

LeBron refused to even think about it.

"I haven't even really looked at it as just one game away," he said. "I look at it as this is our next game. As crazy as it sounds, I haven't got caught up in it."

The Heat kept their focus on this single game and dominated it. By the second half they had opened up a twenty-seven-point lead, and went on to win the game, the series, and the championship without much drama, 121–106. LeBron delivered twenty-six points, eleven rebounds, and thirteen assists and was named MVP of The Finals. With the win in hand, LeBron, Dwyane, and Chris spent the final 3:01 of the game on the bench, cheering on their teammates and celebrating, hugging everyone in sight.

"You know, I dreamed about this opportunity and this moment for a long time, including last night, including today," LeBron said. "My dream has become a reality now, and it's the best feeling I ever had.

"The best thing that happened to me last year was us losing The Finals," LeBron continued. "It was the best thing to ever happen to me in my career because basically I got back to the basics. It humbled me. I knew what it was going to have to take, and I was going to have to change as a basketball player, and I was going to have to change as a person to get what I wanted."

He eventually hoisted the trophy above his head and hugged Savannah, his sons, and his mom. Surrounded by the support system that always believed in him, LeBron James was finally a champion.

11

The Return

IF THE 2011–12 SEASON was about the Heat proving they could be champions, then 2012–13 was about proving just how dominant this super team could be. They posted a 66–16 record and there were nights when they crushed opponents—they beat Charlotte by thirty-two, Brooklyn by thirty, Washington by thirty, and Sacramento by twenty-nine.

On February 3, they beat Toronto by fifteen—the start of a twenty-seven-game winning streak that stretched all the way to March 25. During it, LeBron played some of the best basketball of his career. He would go on to win his fourth MVP title and average 26.8 points a game and shoot 56.5 percent from the floor, far higher than he did back in Cleveland.

Not surprisingly, the Heat reached The Finals and matched up against San Antonio, which still had a lineup of star players, including Tim Duncan and Kawhi Leonard, a second-year forward who seemed destined for greatness. It was, in some ways, a rematch for LeBron from his first Finals appearance back in 2007. This one was far more competitive, with the two great teams going back and forth.

San Antonio led 3–2 and thought it had the series won when it led by ten going into the fourth quarter of Game 6. Miami stormed back, though, forced overtime, and pulled out a victory. LeBron had a triple-double of thirty-two points, ten rebounds, and eleven assists. It was one of the most intense games in recent NBA history. Game 7 was no different, a two-point game into the final minute before LeBron scored four late points and Miami won again. To beat a team the caliber of San Antonio was not lost on LeBron.

"Last year when I was sitting up here, with my first championship, I said it was the toughest thing I had ever done," he said. "[I was] absolutely wrong.

This was the toughest championship right here, between the two."

A year later, in June of 2014, the two teams met again. This Heat team wasn't quite as sharp as the previous two years, particularly because Dwyane battled injuries much of the year. They won just fifty-four regular-season games, good but not dominant. They were still able to make The Finals, but once there, it was clear San Antonio was the better team. Motivated by the prior year's loss, the Spurs played brilliant ball and won the title, 4–1.

After the Finals loss, LeBron was peppered with questions about his future. When he came to Miami, he had signed a four-year contract. It was now ending. He and his teammates had reached four Finals and won two championships. He could either stay in Miami and try for another title, or sign with any other team in the league.

He loved Miami and everything the Heat did for him. He also had what he called "unfinished business" somewhere else . . . Cleveland. LeBron felt he had learned how to win a championship while he was in Miami, and if he returned to Cleveland with that knowledge and was able to attract some other great players to join him, then maybe he could try again to bring that long-awaited title to the city.

Speculation raged across the country. Ohio sat on edge. Media wondered if LeBron would really return to a fan base that had burned his jerseys and heckled him when he left. Then on July 11, 2014, LeBron released an essay he wrote in *Sports Illustrated* announcing his choice.

"Before anyone ever cared where I would play basketball, I was a kid from Northeast Ohio," it read. "It's where I walked. It's where I ran. It's where I cried. It's where I bled. It holds a special place in my heart. People there have seen me grow up. I sometimes feel like I'm their son. Their passion can be overwhelming. But it drives me. I want to give them hope when I can. I want to inspire them when I can. My relationship with Northeast Ohio is bigger than basketball. I didn't realize that four years ago. I do now.

"In Northeast Ohio, nothing is given. Everything is earned. You work for what you have.

"I'm ready to accept the challenge. I'm coming home."

With that, LeBron was a Cleveland Cavalier again. Fans again took to the streets, but this time to rejoice. If LeBron was forgiving them, they were forgiving him. The team had struggled without him, regularly finishing in last place. About the only bright spot for Cleveland since LeBron's departure was that it had drafted a talented point guard named Kyrie Irving. Later that summer, with LeBron as bait to draw in new talent, the Cavs traded for a top power forward named Kevin Love. Now LeBron had some excellent players around him. But since he was older and wiser than when he'd orchestrated "The Decision," he didn't promise any titles this time around.

That didn't mean he wasn't determined to give Cleveland a victory party it hadn't experienced since 1964.

Transforming Cleveland from a loser into a champion wasn't going to happen overnight. LeBron knew just having talent wasn't enough to win. He likened his four years in Miami and learning the culture of winning championships to going away to college. Now he was back. And he was willing to teach.

In the fourth game of the season, Cleveland played the Utah Jazz in Salt Lake City. The box score looked good. LeBron scored thirty-one points. Kyrie scored thirty-four. Yet the Cavs lost 102–100, and dropped to 1–3 on the season. The issue? LeBron had just four assists and Kyrie, the point guard whose job includes getting everyone else the ball, had zero. They were scoring points but not working together. That's what cost them the game, and if it kept up, LeBron knew it would prevent them from winning a championship.

"LeBron came up to me and was like, 'You can never have another game with no assists,'" Kyrie told Cleveland.com. "And I was like, 'All right, cool, it won't happen again.' And it hasn't happened since."

That's what LeBron, about to turn thirty, with four MVP and two NBA titles, could provide that he couldn't when he was nineteen. When he spoke to younger teammates, they listened. He knew what he was talking about. They wanted what he had—a winning philosophy and the championship rings to back it up. He, Kyrie, and Kevin slowly formed a partnership.

LeBron felt extremely comfortable in Cleveland. He had continued to spend time in the off-season in Akron and he and his family loved moving back full-time. Everything was familiar. Everything felt right. Zhuri James was born that fall, adding a daughter to the family.

The Cavs' record went from 33–49 the previous season to 53–29 after LeBron rejoined the team, a twenty-game improvement. LeBron's scoring (25.3) and shooting percentages (53.6) both dropped, but he wasn't too concerned with individual statistics. He just wanted to win. By the playoffs, Cleveland was formidable, going 12–2 in the first three rounds to reach The Finals. The downside was Kevin injured his shoulder in round one and was lost for the season.

Then there was their Finals opponent, one of the best teams of all time—the Golden State Warriors—with league MVP Stephen Curry, sharpshooter Klay Thompson, and defensive and rebounding force Draymond Green. The Warriors had gone 67–15, one of the best regular-season team records in NBA history.

Game 1 was at Golden State. Cleveland forced the game to go to overtime, but during the frantic action Kyrie injured his knee. The Warriors not only won the game, Cleveland was without Kyrie for the rest of the series as well. Suddenly it was like the old Cavs, LeBron and a bunch of role players.

Despite that, LeBron rose his level of play to almost superhuman levels. He had thirty-nine points, sixteen rebounds, and eleven assists to lead the Cavs to a Game 2 victory. Then he had forty, twelve, and eight in a Game 3 victory. Without much help, LeBron had Cleveland up 2–1 against the mighty Warriors and their cast of All-Stars. The basketball world was in awe. Could he pull this off? Could he carry the team on his back and get two more victories?

In the end, Golden State had too many great players. Curry was particularly dangerous, but veteran Andre Iguodala, a dynamic weapon off the bench, was also brilliant on both ends. LeBron averaged an amazing 35.8 points, 13.3 rebounds, and 8.8 assists in the series. He averaged 45.7 minutes per game, playing nearly every minute of the series. Yet it wasn't enough. LeBron was so incredible that he was almost named MVP of The Finals despite being on the losing team. Iguodala won it, but when asked what it was like defending LeBron, all he could say was "exhausting."

The loss was disappointing. It also inspired hope. Cleveland proved it could play with Golden State even with all the team injuries. What would happen a year later, if Kyrie and Kevin were healthy and the Cavs added some needed pieces?

"It's never a success if you go out losing," LeBron said. "But I think we put ourselves back where this franchise needs to be, being a contender."

Cleveland was certainly a contender when they returned in the 2015–16 season. They won fifty-seven games in the regular season, and then went 12–2 as they barreled through the Eastern Conference on their way to The Finals.

Golden State wasn't just a contender, though— they were a history-making squad, setting the regular-season record for victories by finishing 73–9. Not even Michael Jordan's Bulls had ever finished a season with single-digit losses. Offensively they were almost impossible to stop, especially when Steph Curry was hitting his shots. Yet in the playoffs they began to stumble, trailing Oklahoma City 3–1 before rallying to win the series and setting up a Finals rematch against Cleveland.

The Cavs were fully healthy and thought they could handle the Warriors' offense. Instead Golden State took a 3–1 series lead, winning all of its games by double digits. Even with Kyrie and Kevin playing, the Warriors were dominating like they had the year prior. No team had ever come back from a 3–1 deficit in the NBA Finals. To change that, Cleveland would need to make some history of its own and win three consecutive games against a Golden State team that lost just nine times in the entire regular season.

LeBron and the Cavs refused to give up hope. "It's do or die," he said.

In Game 5, the Cavs chose "do." LeBron scored forty-one. Kyrie scored forty-one. It was enough for Cleveland to ruin what Golden State fans thought would be a championship celebration on their home court. Back home in Game 6, LeBron was once again a mighty force, repeating his forty-one-point performance, and Cleveland won again, setting up the historic Game 7 that ended with LeBron's memorable block from chapter 1.

Against all odds, after a fifty-two-year drought, Cleveland was a champion at last.

"I came back for a reason," LeBron said as fans back home rushed into the street to celebrate.

"I came back to bring a championship to our city. I knew what I was capable of doing. I knew what I learned in the years that I was gone . . . I knew I had the right ingredients and the right blueprint to help this franchise get back to a place that we've never been. That's what it was all about."

Three days later, the city of Cleveland held a parade to celebrate the area's first major professional championship since 1964. One million people came out to enjoy it, lining downtown streets and hanging out of office windows and parking decks. It was a party out of Cleveland's wildest dreams, and in the middle of it all, as he and his family rode in the back of a truck, soaking in the cheers, was the best basketball player in the world.

"Hey, we did it," LeBron said to the crowd. "Let's get ready for next year."

12

Legacy

IT WAS LEBRON'S DREAM to give Northeast Ohio a championship to call its own. It was his dream to bring attention to the region, whether it was as a kid trying to win an AAU national title for Akron, or a high school national title for St. Vincent-St. Mary, or sparking Cleveland to hold a million-person victory parade.

Sports are sports, though. Victories are fleeting. Celebrations are fun, but they end.

As his fame and power and influence grew, he wanted to do much more than that. He wanted to support and elevate the community that had given him so much.

Through the years LeBron had been a major booster for the Boys & Girls Clubs of America, including donating one thousand computers to their sites across the country. He started the After-School All-Stars in Akron for kids who didn't have the safest home lives. He worked with the ONEXONE foundation, which focuses on important issues affecting many children: hunger, health, education, and a lack of clean water and safe places to play. He even supported the Children's Defense Fund, a Washington, DC–based nonprofit that advocates for child welfare around the world.

Then there were LeBron's many small efforts. He worked with HGTV to rehab homes in Northeast Ohio. He promoted reading in elementary and middle schools. He held basketball camps and encouraged athletes at all levels: youth, high school, college, and the Special Olympics. He funded an initiative that taught kids how to write computer-language code.

He donated millions of dollars to his old high school. He constructed the LeBron James Clubhouse in Akron, which gave local kids a place to play and study after school, and fed many of them a hot meal each day. It was often their only full meal. He worked with the University of Akron to guarantee one thousand scholarships to local students, making sure they didn't have to give up on the dream of college just because they might not have enough money.

"It means so much because, as a kid growing up in the inner city and [for] a lot of African American kids, you don't really think past high school," James said. "You don't really know your future. You hear high school all the time, and you graduate high school and then you never think past that because either it's not possible or your family's not financially stable to be able to support a kid going to college."

As the seasons continued after his return to Cleveland, he was focused on making an impact both on the court and off. "I'm able to do so many things because I'm actually there, hands on, with my foundation," LeBron said. "I'm able to uplift the youth in my community and also in other communities."

LeBron also made a point to be the best father he could be for his three children. Growing up, he struggled accepting that his father had abandoned him and his mother. He knew the challenges and the pain of not having a dad around. He promised himself that when he had children, he would always be there for them and his wife.

He was often seen taking his kids to the park, bringing them to hang around the Cavs practice facility, and especially taking pride while cheering on Bronny's and Bryce's basketball games. Both showed considerable ability and LeBron tried to be at every game possible, even if he caused a stir in the crowd. As much as he wanted to be a normal dad, there were times it was clear he was still LeBron James the superstar. Once, before one of Bronny's summer basketball games, LeBron went out on the court and entertained the fans with some dunks.

"Just breaking the mold, that's all," James told Cleveland.com about not just being a hands-on dad, but also serving as a role model to other young fathers as well. "I wanted to be a part of the statistics that breaks the mold of fathers running out on their kids. I knew from day one that wasn't going to be me. To have a family and be there for them and be there on a day-to-day basis is important. It means a lot to me and I know it means a lot to my kids."

On the court, he was still at the top of his game. He continued to score points and haul in rebounds, climbing the list of the all-time greats. He delivered victories and fun. His shoe line with Nike became iconic. But unfortunately, winning another championship in Cleveland proved unattainable.

After winning seventy-three games but losing The Finals to Cleveland in 2016, Golden State made a big addition in the offseason and added free agent Kevin Durant, who, along with LeBron and Steph Curry, was one of the three best players in the NBA. The Warriors went from nearly impossible to beat to truly impossible to beat.

In 2017, Cleveland returned to The Finals to defend its title and lost to Golden State, 4–1. In 2018, it went back again (LeBron's eighth consecutive Finals appearance, dating back to his first year in Miami). Golden State swept them 4–0. LeBron was incredible in each series. It didn't matter. The Warriors were just too much. Golden State was the better team.

It was time, LeBron believed, to try something new. In the summer of 2018, he decided to become a free agent again. After the fanfare of his past free agency moves, LeBron decided to handle this process quietly, or as quietly as the best basketball player in the world can. He signed a five-year contract with the Los Angeles Lakers. LeBron felt his job in

Cleveland was done and he was ready to add a new chapter to his legacy.

The first season, 2018–19, was a challenge, as the young team failed to play together and LeBron battled injuries. After appearing in eight consecutive NBA Finals, LeBron didn't even reach the playoffs. It proved to be the first time since he was just twenty years old that his team didn't make the postseason. LeBron was frustrated.

Back in Cleveland, the Cavaliers fans held no hard feelings. There would be no burned jerseys when LeBron announced he was leaving. They understood and appreciated what he had given them.

"I came back because I felt like I had some unfinished business," LeBron said. "To be able to be a part of a championship team with the team that we had and in the fashion that we had is something I will always remember. Honestly, I think we'll all remember that. It ended a drought for Cleveland of fifty-plus years."

However, before leaving Ohio, he wanted to accomplish his most ambitious charitable goal to date. In the summer of 2018, he partnered with the Akron public school system to open a brand-new school—the I Promise School. It began with just two classes, but will expand to include kindergarten through eighth grade. It offers free tuition, free uniforms, and free books.

Remembering his own days growing up with a poor, single mother and often not having enough to eat, LeBron ensured that the school's cafeteria also provides free breakfast, lunch, and snacks, plus a food pantry for kids who might need to bring something home to eat later. And if students don't have a ride to school—as LeBron dealt with in third and fourth grades—the school provides free transportation to any student who lives within two miles, and all students receive a free bicycle. Any kid who makes it through I Promise automatically earns a full scholarship to the University of Akron. And in an effort to support their families, the school offers free education for parents to be able to come back and earn a high school degree.

This day and this accomplishment—not scoring points or winning titles—was LeBron's greatest achievement.

"For kids, in general, all they want to know is that someone cares," LeBron told CNN. "And when they walk through that door, I hope they know someone cares."

Yes, for the kids in Akron it was clear that someone cared . . . another former kid from Akron who set out to change the world and has done it, on the court and, even more importantly, off of it.

Instant
Replay

GAME 7
FINALS 2016
CLE	GS
89	89
4TH	1:55

LEBRON TRAILS BEHIND AS GOLDEN STATE GOES ON A FAST BREAK.

LEBRON CHASES AFTER ANDRE IGUODALA.

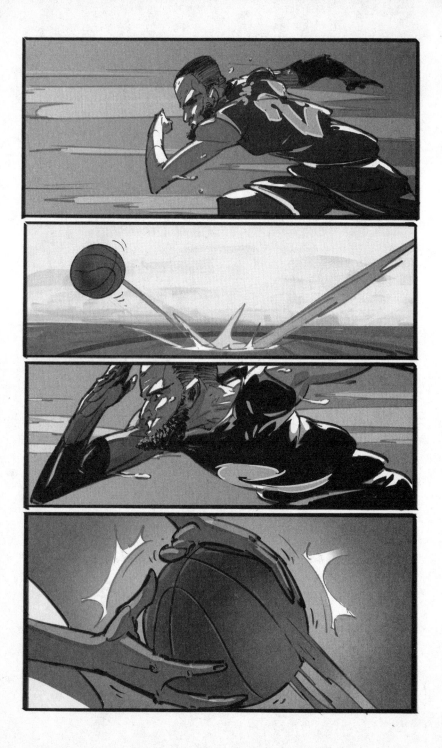

LEBRON'S DREAM OF BRINGING AN NBA CHAMPIONSHIP TO CLEVELAND COMES TRUE!

The Nonstop Sports Action Continues!

EPIC ATHLETES
STEPHEN CURRY

1

Underdog

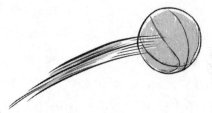

TWENTY THOUSAND CLEVELAND CAVALIERS
fans stood inside Quicken Loans Arena and tried
to distract Stephen Curry. They stomped their feet.
They waved their arms. They cupped their hands up
to their faces and screamed.

It was Game 6 of the 2015 NBA Finals, and
Cleveland's J. R. Smith had just drained a three-
pointer. A Golden State lead that only minutes
before had stretched to thirteen points was now
just four, 101–97. There were 29.0 seconds remaining, still enough time for the Cavaliers to mount a

comeback. Golden State led the series 3–2 and was trying to win the franchise's first NBA title in forty years. The Warriors wanted to end the series right then, in this game, and avoid having to play a decisive Game 7. They didn't want to give Cleveland superstar LeBron James another chance to win it all.

Cleveland had all the momentum. It was up to Curry to stop it, win the game, and grab the championship that he had spent a lifetime dreaming about.

Golden State had won sixty-seven games in the regular season, among the most by any team in NBA history. Behind Curry and teammate Klay Thompson, dubbed the "Splash Brothers" for the way so many of their long three-pointers splashed through the net, the team had cruised to The Finals with a 12–3 record. It was expected to beat Cleveland handily, especially after one of the Cavs' stars, Kyrie Irving, was lost to injury.

Instead, LeBron raised his level of play and Cleveland took two of the first three games. To make matters worse, Steph, the best player in the league that season, was in a slump. His usually reliable shot was off. At the end of the Game 2 loss, he'd shot just two of fifteen from three-point range. He'd even tossed up an air ball, missing the rim altogether.

"Shots I normally make . . . I knew as soon as they left my hand that they were off," Steph explained. "That doesn't usually happen."

In the media, there was talk that Steph wasn't tough enough for the big games and the pressure of the NBA Finals was getting to him. He had shaken that off and returned to form in Games 4, 5, and now Game 6. The Warriors clawed back and took the lead in the series. They couldn't imagine it all coming undone in the last minute.

Everything rested on the slim shoulders of Steph Curry, who had been fouled and awarded two free throws. If he missed one or both of the shots from the line, Cleveland still had a chance. If he hit them, Golden State was almost assuredly going to win.

With the pressure mounting and the noise of all those Cavaliers fans raining down on him, Steph walked to the free-throw line. For years he had dreamed of and practiced for this moment. His entire life he'd been told over and over the same thing by coaches, scouts, and the media—that he would never be good enough to be a great college star or NBA player, let alone the MVP of the entire league.

Too small, they said. Too short, they claimed. Too little, they argued.

Hungry for More EPIC ATHLETES?
Look Out for These Superstar
Biographies, in Stores Now!

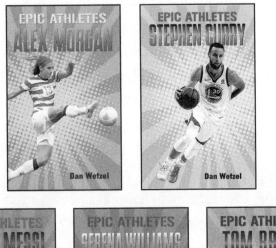

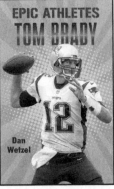